GRATITUDE TO MY ANCESTORS ON WHOSE SHOULDERS I STAND TALL

EVANGELINE N. ASAFOR, PHD.

©2019 by Evangeline N. Asafor. All rights reserved.

IEM PRESS (PO Box 831001, Richardson, TX 75080) functions only as book publisher. As such, the ultimate design, content, editorial accuracy, and views expressed or implied in this work are those of the author. No part of this publication may be reproduced, stored in a retrieval system, or transmitted in any way by any means—electronic, mechanical, photocopy, recording, or otherwise—without the prior permission of the copyright holder, except as provided by USA copyright law. Unless otherwise noted, all Scriptures are taken from the Holy Bible, New International Version®, NIV®. Copyright © 1973, 1978, 1984, 2011 by Biblica, Inc.™ Used by permission of Zondervan. All rights reserved worldwide. www.zondervan.com
ISBN

ISBN 10: 1-947662-62-7
ISBN 13: 978-1-947662-62-9

Library of Congress Catalog Card Number: 2019916656

DEDICATION

This book is specially dedicated to my ancestors from Akum, Pinyin, and, Kom villages of the North West Region of Cameroon near the West Coast of Central Africa. On the shoulders of these great parentages, I have been blessed to stand tall in wisdom and understanding of our cultural, spiritual, moral, and social values. To my luminary father, I say "Papa, your meaningful and purpose-driven life help mold me and put the final polish on my life. You are a living proof that the value of life is in its donation, not in its duration and we are all created to make a difference, not a living. Papa, you impacted so many lives by donating your time and services to many people and many causes. Sometimes, I am intrigued that you went to be with the Lord at age 65. May your soul continue to rest in peace till we meet again to part no more. Amen!

ACKNOWLEDGEMENTS

Thanks to my Creator, Jehovah God, who knew me before forming me in my mother's womb, who made me fearfully and wonderfully, who has been with me every step of the way protecting and empowering me. To Him I give all the Glory!

To my luminary Papa whose love, dedication, resilience, and, wisdom helped nourish my roots and molded me into the purpose driven woman I am today. To my sweet mother whose discipline, love, wisdom, and resilience gave me the strength and shaped me into the strong and dedicated woman I am today. To my maternal grandmother whose discipline, proverbs, love and humility laid a solid foundation for me, shaping my life for the challenging future ahead of me. To my village elders, I must applaud you for teaching me the ways of wisdom and warning me never to use the phrase "straight from the horse's mouth" in reference to anything said by an elder. Gratitude to all our neighbors now resting in the Lord who disciplined me (under the pretext that it took a village to raise a child) just when I thought I could get away with mischievous acts in the absence of my parents.

I come before you all to acknowledge that I stand tall today because at one point or the other, one of you selflessly offered your shoulders as support for me to grow and learn. With a humble spirit, and a heart full of gratitude, I thank God almighty for every single one of you and pray that your souls continue to rest in perfect peace. Amen! Amen! Amen!

TABLE OF CONTENTS

Forword..vii
Introduction 1
Chapter 1: Celebrating My Roots 3
Chapter 2: What I Can See Sitting, You Can't See Standing on the Tallest Mountain 9
Chapter 3: Village Locusts Abomination/Festival 14
Chapter 4: Fireside Crash Course in Marriage...18
Chapter 5: Material Support in Time of Need 22
Chapter 6: Wisdom is Not Hidden..26
Chapter 7: You Must Dig Your Well Before You Get Thirsty 29
Chapter 8: Other People Are More Important Than You........................32
Chapter 9: Intelligence Is Better Than Power..35
Chapter 10: Tracing your Lineage to Complete Your Family Tree 38
Chapter 11: The Village Story with Three Titles 43
Chapter 12 : I Was a Second World War Veteran 47
Chapter 13: Go where You are Celebrated Not Tolerated 50
Chapter 14: The Importance of Time and Opportunity 53
Chapter 15: Lessons from the Caterpillar 55
Chapter 16: Let Dogs Delight to Bark and Bite...60
Chapter 17: Lion and Eagle Leadership Attitude 63
Chapter 18: Loving is Giving 67

Chapter 19: The Story of the Hunt Will Always Glorify the Hunter 70

Chapter 20: If Everyone is a Drummer, There Will Be No Dancers 73

Chapter 21: Love Should Not Be the Foundation of a Godly Marriage 77

Chapter 22: The Purpose of Your Existence 82

Chapter 23: Avoiding a Fight is a Mark of Honor 86

Chapter 24: A White Man Has Landed on the Moon 90

Chapter 25: Leadership is an Action, Not a Position.................................. 95

Chapter 26: If You Fail to Plan, Then Plan to Fail 102

Chapter 27: If You Think Education is Expensive, Try Ignorance 106

Chapter 28: You Cannot Teach Without Learning 110

Chapter 29: Success Means Obedience to God and
Godly Obedience to Others 114

Chapter 30: It Takes a Village to Raise a Child 119

Chapter 31: The Power of the Tongue 123

Chapter 32: A Mother Understands What a Child Does Not Say 128

Chapter 33: Silence is an African Value 134

Chapter 34: No One is Exempted from Pain and Suffering.................... 138

Chapter 35: When You See Success, Don't Get Jealous — Get Curious 144

Chapter 36: Seek Christ's Wisdom, Not King Solomon's 147

Chapter 37: The Rights and Responsibilities of Twins and
Their Parents 155

Chapter 38: Heaven Helps Those Who Can't Help Themselves 160

Chapter 39: The Importance of Seeking Wise Counsel 163

Chapter 40: SPECIAL ACKNOWLEDGEMENT 167

FOREWORD

Dr. Asafor's work in this book is a brilliant and refreshing telling of the upbringing of an African female child in the country of Cameroon. As a child of the Caribbean Diaspora, this telling has filled a gap in understanding of what life could have been like *sans* the terrible institution which robbed us in the Diaspora of our own African story. Reading this enthralling work by Dr. Asafor gave me an insight that I could not have gotten from reading any other work on growing up in an African country, simply because I know her personally and it became abundantly clear where her wealth of wisdom, compassion, her sense of duty and love of mankind originated — the village of Akum on the West Coast of Central Africa, Cameroon.

From reading this wonderful work, I posit that luminary Papa, Joseph Nkwenti Asafor, is the star of this book. His knowledge, wisdom, and strong faith come across so clearly. He was an erudite instructor to his children, the school where he taught, and to his community. He was filled with kindness and compassion and understood the importance of educating girls as well as boys where he was quoted as saying in Chapter 27: "Educating the girl child is not a waste of money; it is the education of a nation" and "If you think education is expensive, try ignorance." His wisdom only seemed to be outstripped by his faith in characteristics. He was a phenomenal repository of ancient and new wisdom and dispensed all freely to those he encountered as described in the book. May he continue to rest in the bosom of the Most High God.

All the wisdom in this work can be summed up by a passage in Chapter 6 *Wisdom is Not Hidden* where Grandpa Tanyi Mbah's fireside nights of wisdom advised the youngsters gathered to listen, "If a child washes his hands really clean, he can eat from the same bowl as the elders. While eating, if he shuts his mouth and opens his ears and mind, he can learn a thing or two."

We are all children seeking wisdom and knowledge on this life's journey and must wash our hands. This work is a must-read by all in the Diaspora; all parents; those with aspirations of being parents, particularly those planning to take on the influential mantle of "father".

Thank you, Dr. Asafor, for sharing this exquisite story. This work is a true tribute to your ancestors. May your faith and knowledge continue to soar to the heavens.

Linda A. Greene, L.L.B. Hons.

INTRODUCTION

When I was born on that faithful morning at the Akum Health Center, my parents were overjoyed. I was the seventh child of the family and the sixth daughter. Unlike my other siblings, my naming was delayed. My luminary Papa wrote a letter to my oldest sister Emmerentia announcing my birth and giving her the honor to name me. He informed my sister that Mama had given birth to a baby girl who is as beautiful as she was and looks so much like her when she was born. My sister received the letter, was very happy, and took the ten-hour bus journey to Akum to see and name her precious baby sister. When she got to the village and saw me, she at once named me *Evangeline*. She had prayed and asked God for guidance and when she saw me, God dropped this strange name in her spirit, a name she had never heard or seen anywhere. My sweet mother, my luminary Papa and my elder sister came into a prayer of agreement that beautiful baby *Evangeline* will grow up to impact nations and be a *bearer of good tidings*.

I migrated to the United States of America in November of 2000. One of my memorable moments was the day I was sworn in as a U.S. citizen! I made a promise to myself to be an asset to this great nation, not a liability. I have worked as a Licensed Practical Nurse since 2005 in the areas of Rehabilitation, Hospice, and Home Health while attending school towards my greater passion as a criminal justice professional. I hold a Ph.D. in Criminal Justice with a specialization in Online Teaching in Higher Education. My Ph.D. thesis is on Financial Accountability in U.S. Nonprofit Organizations. I have published three books in the last two years: *My letters of Gratitude to Jehovah God, My Sweet Mother's Doctrines of Gratitude and Her Final Rest with Jehovah God*, and *Gratitude as a Facilitator of Other Virtues in Jehovah God*.

I pray that God almighty will continue to keep me as the apple of His eye and protect me with the shadow of His wings so that I can be who He created me to be and to live up to the name *Evangeline*. With a humble spirit and a grateful heart, I thank God for my Sister Mummy Emmerentia and for the beautiful name I carry, Amen. Dearest Ancestors, you taught me by your actions and by your words how to add virtue to my faith, knowledge to my virtue, self-control to my knowledge, steadfastness to my self-control, godliness to my steadfastness, brotherly kindness to my godliness, and love to my brotherly kindness. Thank you, sweet Mother, luminary Papa, and all my other ancestors. May your souls continue to rest in peace. Amen.

May my intriguing journey on the shoulder of my ancestors, bless, inspire and entertain you. Amen!

CHAPTER ONE
CELEBRATING MY ROOTS

With a grateful heart and a humble spirit, I must start by celebrating my original and everlasting roots in God almighty for creating me in His own very image. How comforting to know that I am God's masterpiece beautifully and wonderfully made! I thank God for sending me into the world through ancestors from across four different African villages blessed with a rich spiritual and cultural heritage. My paternal grandparents where from the village of Pinyin. My father was raised by family members in the village of Akum.

My maternal great grandparents were from the village of Kom and my maternal grandparents were from the village of Awing and Akum. Together and at different times, these great ancestors accumulated and shared knowledge and wisdom generously, which has been passed down generation after generation. Generation after generation, they all agreed on these six basic truths:

1. Seek first the Kingdom of God and His righteousness.
2. Never forget where you came from; celebrate your roots.
3. Respect yourself and others.
4. Seek wisdom and use it cautiously.
5. Watch your tongue always.
6. Guard against the spirit of fear, for if you give your fear wings, it will fly away with your dream.

Africa is not only a very rich continent when it comes to natural resources, but it's super rich when you talk of cultures, diversity, landscapes, and most of all, ancestral stories, riddles and jokes. Growing up in a village in Cameroon near the west coast of Central Africa was the best childhood any child could ever ask for! The highlights of village life were intertwined in birth celebrations, traditional marriage celebrations, death celebrations, 10-mile-long walks to the farms, and storytelling time by the fireside. As a child growing up in the village where elders were God's special agents, respect was huge, demanded and reinforced.

The penalties for disrespecting others, especially your elders, could range from firewood fetching, water fetching, flogging, and other life-threatening consequences. It was a sign of disrespect to question the facts of any story told by the elders. Growing up in Akum village in Cameroon, you could be beaten or given another form of punishment such as filling the drum with water from the stream or going out to fetch for firewood for any of the following crimes:

1. Crying before a beating, crying after being beaten, not crying after being beaten
2. Standing while the elders are seated, sitting while the elders stand, walking around aimlessly where the elders are seated
3. Talking back to an elder, not replying to an elder
4. Singing after being admonished or grumbling after a beating
5. Not greeting visitors or greeting visitors too quickly
6. Crying to go with the visitors when the visitors are leaving
7. Refusing to eat as a sign of discontentment
8. Coming back home after sunset
9. Eating at the neighbor's home without permission from your parents
10. Generally being moody or generally being too excited.
11. Fighting with your age mate and losing or fighting with your age mate and winning
12. Eating too slowly, too quickly or too much
13. Whistling while the elders were sleeping

14. Looking at the visitors while they are eating
15. Stumbling and falling when walking

We survived all the village rules and regulations and have many stories to tell like Grandpa Mufor-Ngu's Second World War stories! These stories were many — some intriguing, some frightful, some inspiring, and some doubtful. I remember my grandpa telling a group of anxious listeners that the truth and importance of any story lies within you, the listener. And that it was up to you, the listener to make good use of any story told to you by the elders.

What the Holy Bible says about ancestral wisdom:

- **Job 12:12 -** Is not wisdom found among the aged? Does not long-life bring understanding?

- **Proverbs 1:8-9 -** Listen, my son, to your father's instruction and do not forsake your mother's teaching. They are a garland to grace your head and a chain to adorn your neck.

- **Proverbs 2:11-12 -** Discretion will protect you, and understanding will guard you. Wisdom will save you from the ways of wicked men, from men whose words are perverse.

- **Proverbs 3:13-15 -** Blessed are those who find wisdom, those who gain understanding, for she is more profitable than silver and yields better returns than gold. She is more precious than rubies; nothing you desire can compare with her.

- **Proverbs 3:21-23 -** My son, do not let wisdom and understanding out of your sight, preserve sound judgment and discretion; they will be life for you, an ornament to grace your neck. Then you will go on your way in safety, and your foot will not stumble.

✠ **Proverbs 4:1-27-** Listen, my sons, to a father's instruction; pay attention and gain understanding. I give you sound learning, so do not forsake my teaching. For I, too, was a son to my father, still tender, and cherished by my mother. Then, he taught me, and he said to me, "Take hold of my words with all your heart; keep my commands, and you will live.

Get wisdom, get understanding; do not forget my words or turn away from them. Do not forsake wisdom, and she will protect you; love her, and she will watch over you. The beginning of wisdom is this: get wisdom. Though it cost all you have, get understanding. Cherish her, and she will exalt you; embrace her, and she will honor you. She will give you a garland to grace your head and present you with a glorious crown." Listen, my son, accept what I say, and the years of your life will be many.

I instruct you in the way of wisdom and lead you along straight paths. When you walk, your steps will not be hampered; when you run, you will not stumble. Hold on to instruction, do not let it go; guard it well, for it is your life. Do not set foot on the path of the wicked or walk in the way of evildoers. Avoid it, do not travel on it; turn from it and go on your way. For they cannot rest until they do evil; they are robbed of sleep till they make someone stumble. They eat the bread of wickedness and drink the wine of violence.

The path of the righteous is like the morning sun, shining ever brighter till the full light of day. But the way of the wicked is like deep darkness; they do not know what makes them stumble.

My son pay attention to what I say; turn your ear to my words. Do not let them out of your sight, keep them within your heart; for they are life to those who find them and health to one's whole body. Above all else, guard your heart, for everything you do flows from it. Keep your mouth free of perversity; keep corrupt talk far from your lips. Let your eyes look straight ahead; fix your gaze directly before you. Give careful thought to the paths for your feet and be steadfast in all your ways. Do not turn to the right or the left; keep your foot from evil.

- **Proverbs 23:22 -** Listen to your father, who gave you life, and do not despise your mother when she is old.

- **Titus 2:1-5 -** But as for you, teach what accords with sound doctrine. Older men are to be sober-minded, dignified, self-controlled, sound in faith, in love, and in steadfastness. Older women likewise are to be reverent in behavior, not slanderers or slaves to much wine. They are to teach what is good, and so train the young women to love their husbands and children, to be self-controlled, pure, working at home, kind, and submissive to their own husbands, that the word of God may not be reviled.

CHAPTER TWO
WHAT I CAN SEE SITTING, YOU CANNOT SEE STANDING ON THE TALLEST MOUNTAIN

I am about to share a secret known to only three people and I hope I can trust you to keep this secret, too. Growing up, our parents were very strict and we as children could hardly get away with anything. In the absence of one parent, the other parent will magically develop an extra pair of eyes and ears. However, we were blessed to have a grandmother who lived less than ten miles from us and will, every now and then, make the two-hour journey on foot to come spend a few days with us. We loved having her around because she always came bearing gifts. Also, when she was around, our mother's extra pairs of eyes and ears will reduce by half and we could have some real fun and get away with a few village crimes.

When Grandma came visiting when I was about five years old, I was so happy to have her around that I basically followed her everywhere she went. As I followed along, I realized that every morning before plucking a guava stem to use as chewing stick for her teeth, she will first throw something into the coffee farm. I asked her on several occasions, and she won't tell why she did that. Being the inquisitive young girl, I kept asking her over and over and decided to spend time during the day throwing stones into the coffee farm instead of doing chores. That got my Grandma aggravated enough and she took me for a walk and explained to me that she was using the stones to keep track of time. She explained to me that whenever she was coming to spend time with us, she will put stones in her back equivalent to the length of time she wanted to stay.

Every morning she will get rid of one small stone and when she had one left in her back, she will pack up her bags, say her goodbyes and leave the next day. Wow! My curious mind went to work! I was as excited as if I had single-handedly discovered a new planet full of innovations. My Grandma warned me to keep what she had told me a secret and I promised to keep the secret. Later that evening, I was scolded for telling my older sister that I was keeping Grandma's secret and will never tell anyone. I did not understand why she will get so mad at me for promising my sister not to tell her secret. The little warrior in me spoke, I listened and acted.

To get back at Grandma, I sneaked into her raffia made bag and stumbled right on the small stones tied in a very old piece of clothing. I untied the piece of cloth and it had four small stones left. I removed two, neatly tied it back and kept those two stones buried behind the kitchen and marked the spot with a handmade cross. Two days after that, grandma had finished throwing the last two stones and it was time to slowly walk home. It felt sad seeing her leave, but it was too late to change anything. I prayed to God where I had buried the two stones and that spot became my prayer spot.

Not long after that, my father fell sick and my Grandma came to see us again and brought gifts as usual. While with us, she spoiled us with her cooking and interesting village stories, riddles and jokes. This time, she behaved herself and when everyone had gone to the farm, I stayed to assist my father who was feeling much better. While he took his afternoon nap, I sneaked into my grandma's bag to check how much longer she had with us. I discovered that the cloth only had two stones left, so I added one stone.

Three days later, my Grandma left. I did not feel as bad as I did before, and I thanked God for making her spend one extra day with us. The warrior in me was now getting restless and I decided to go looking for small stones that looked exactly like the one I had left. I was able to get about ten of such by the very next day. For the next one year, the length of Grandma's stay was all on me. Thinking I was now the best at my game, I let my guard down and my sister caught me searching grandma's bag. I was toast.

The punishment for searching anyone's bag without their knowledge, let alone your grandma's bag, was so severe and almost life-threatening. Rather than go down for trying to steal from Grandma, I told my sister the secret and we had a deal for me to do her chores for the rest of my life. I reluctantly agreed to the deal. I worked for my sister for a few months until my Grandma visited again, one day before I received the First Holy Communion.

Before I left that evening for my three-mile walk to the St. Pius IX Catholic Church for confession before receiving holy communion, Grandma pulled me aside to shock me with the news that she was aware of all my sins. She declared that she knew I was the one taking out and replacing stones in her bag! She told me that she was probably born at night, but not last night! She added that what she can see sitting down, I probably cannot see standing on the tallest mountain! I was beyond myself and begged for mercy! She forgave me and asked me to go to God and ask for forgiveness. I did repent and God forgave me. It remained a secret between my Grandma, my sister, and myself till now.

May the soul of my loving and forgiving Grandma continue to rest in peace. Amen!

What the Holy Bible says about ancestral wisdom

- **Job 12:12 -** Is not wisdom found among the aged? Does not long-life bring understanding?

- **Proverbs 1:8-9 -** Listen, my son, to your father's instruction and do not forsake your mother's teaching. They are a garland to grace your head and a chain to adorn your neck.

➤ **Proverbs 2:11-12** - Discretion will protect you, and understanding will guard you. Wisdom will save you from the ways of wicked men, from men whose words are perverse.

➤ **Proverbs 3:13-15** - Blessed are those who find wisdom, those who gain understanding, for she is more profitable than silver and yields better returns than gold. She is more precious than rubies; nothing you desire can compare with her.

➤ **Proverbs 3:21-23** - My son, do not let wisdom and understanding out of your sight, preserve sound judgment and discretion; they will be life for you, an ornament to grace your neck. Then you will go on your way in safety, and your foot will not stumble.

CHAPTER THREE
VILLAGE LOCUSTS
ABOMINATION/FESTIVAL

It was one morning in the middle of July 1979 when the entire village woke up to a dark sky filled with flying insects never seen before by most of us kids. It was a frightening but intriguing sight to watch these insects descend on trees, crops and any green vegetation in uncountable numbers. Words spread around the village and the villagers all came out to harvest the insects from the crops. We were told this brand of grasshoppers were called locusts.

> *Locusts are certain species of short-horned grasshoppers in the family Acrididae that have a swarming phase. These insects are usually solitary, but under certain circumstances, they become more abundant and change their behavior and habits, becoming gregarious. They form bands of wingless nymphs, which later become swarms of winged adults. Both the bands and the swarms move around and rapidly strip fields and cause damage to crops. The adults are powerful fliers; they can travel great distances, consuming most of the green vegetation wherever the swarm settles.*

The village women even had songs to lament and celebrate these insects. By the next day, these insects were bottled and sold to those passing by in cars. Villages also fried and feasted on these insects to fried and feasted upon. Fried locusts with a little bit of salt and pepper tasted really yummy. For the next six days, the villagers harvested these insects and on the morning of day six, the story had gone viral and more people from nearby villages headed to our village to harvest some locusts as well, but behold, the remaining ones had disappeared without a trace overnight. The trees were left bare and the crops had no leaves left. The locust festival suddenly ended. Those who had sold their previous catch hoping to catch more the following day were left disappointed. Fortunately, for my household, we had enough left to dry and save for future consumption. I ate so much locusts I got sick in the stomach.

A month after the unannounced disappearance of the locusts, my mother fried the last batch of the smoked locusts in palm oil with a little bit of pepper and we all sat by the fireside to enjoy it with some roasted plantains. In the middle of the celebration, my father stopped and asked us a strange question, "Children, what did you learn from the locusts?" We all laughed and gave some silly answers. My father then went on to say, "Now listen very carefully, these are some lessons to draw from the locusts:

1. They have no leader or captain so they must be self-motivated.
2. They did not come in a car or plane, so they must be self-directed.
3. They came at the same time, and left at the same time, so they must be self-disciplined.
4. Even when we started catching and eating them, they never gave up, so they are determined."

My father ended the story by telling us children to be self-motivated, self-directed, self-disciplined, and determined like the locusts. Papa, thanks for your wisdom and patience. May your soul continue to rest in peace. Amen!

What the NIV of the Holy Bible says about locusts, self-motivation, self-discipline, and determination

- **Proverbs 30:27**: The locusts have no king yet go they forth all of them by bands.

▲ **Exodus 10:15**: For they covered the face of the whole earth, so that the land was darkened; and they did eat every herb of the land, and all the fruit of the trees which the hail had left: and there remained not any green thing in the trees, or in the herbs of the field, through all the land of Egypt.

▲ **Job 12:12:** Is not wisdom found among the aged? Does not long-life bring understanding?

▲ **Proverbs 2:**11-12: Discretion will protect you, and understanding will guard you. Wisdom will save you from the ways of wicked men, from men whose words are perverse.

▲ **Proverbs 3:13-15**: Blessed are those who find wisdom, those who gain understanding, for she is more profitable than silver and yields better returns than gold. She is more precious than rubies; nothing you desire can compare with her.

CHAPTER FOUR
FIRESIDE CRASH COURSE IN MARRIAGE

When my brother Njilu was busy with the other boys his age listening to Grandpa Mufor-Ngu's heroic world war stories, I was also sitting with a bunch of other older girls from the neighborhood by the fireside next to my Grandma Ngumah listening to wise counsel for making marriage work in the future. I was only ten years old and already had to listen to the boring lectures on marriage! I had no choice but to listen with an attitude of gratitude. Otherwise, there was a consequence for not listening.

Grandma will always start her marriage lesson with "God created marriage, it's a school founded by God and requires hard work and dedication. It's also a school where you will never graduate. It's a school with little to no break or a free period. Marriage is a school where dropping out or being kicked out was not really God's plan for marriage. It's a school you will have to attend every day of your life the moment you pick your partner, or he picks you. In the classroom of marriage, you need the following utensils: love, trust, acceptance, tolerance, understanding, blessings, faith, communication, respect, humility and you need to be alive."

When I listened to these courses on marriage over and over, I kept thinking how I could escape such a demanding school. When I was fortunate at the age of twelve to get admission into the all-girls secondary school about twelve miles from my village on scholarship, I couldn't thank God enough. While at this all-girls secondary boarding school, I got excited at the idea of becoming a Reverend Sister and not having to deal with the complicated school of marriage. I got really interested in the school of sisterhood and at the age of fourteen, I was given an opportunity over the summer to visit the convent, spend two weeks with the nuns and figure out if sisterhood was my calling. The first two days were not too bad, but by day five, I had it bright and clear that the school of marriage was not nearly as complicated as being a nun. I was a very excited happy-go-lucky young girl and the convent had absolutely no place for such excitement! You couldn't even gossip about something good!

The meals were small, and you were reminded that man does not live by bread alone but by what comes from the mouth of the Lord. At the end of two weeks, it was clear that if I became a nun, lack of excitement and too much prayer would eventually kill me. I gave up on that adventure and held my Grandma's doctrines of marriage close to my heart. To God be all the Glory! Grandma, thanks for your dedication and patience. May your soul continue to rest in peace. Amen!

What the Holy Bible says about ancestral wisdom

- **Job 12:12** - Is not wisdom found among the aged? Does not long-life bring understanding?

- **Proverbs 1:8-9** - Listen, my son, to your father's instruction and do not forsake your mother's teaching. They are a garland to grace your head and a chain to adorn your neck.

- **Proverbs 2:11-12** - Discretion will protect you, and understanding will guard you. Wisdom will save you from the ways of wicked men, from men whose words are perverse.

- **Proverbs 3:13-15** - Blessed are those who find wisdom, those who gain understanding, for she is more profitable than silver and yields better returns than gold. She is more precious than rubies; nothing you desire can compare with her.

⋏ **Proverbs 3:21-23** - My son, do not let wisdom and understanding out of your sight, preserve sound judgment and discretion; they will be life for you, an ornament to grace your neck. Then you will go on your way in safety, and your foot will not stumble.

CHAPTER FIVE
MATERIAL SUPPORT IN TIME OF NEED

Once upon a time, there was a school called St. Julius School Akum. I attended this primary school with my best friend Mambo. It was a typical village school and fighting was a pastime most school children cherished. As part of our village fun, you were either fighting, or supporting those who fought. Somehow, the fun was for all! Unfortunately for me, my grandmother and my parents preached walking away from a physical fight and, therefore, forbade us from ever fighting. The consequences of fighting they said could be very severe and life-threatening.

We were constantly warned against fighting and even told that fighting was a sign that we were dishonoring God, our forefathers and the family name. No shame to our family. No fighting in school. I used to pray to God to help my parents and grandparents see the pleasure of fighting and proving your courage and becoming a leader. I gave up praying for an opportunity to fight and just started enjoying watching others fight. I was constantly made fun for being too weak and too scared to fight and would probably not have a husband in the future. One of the girls making fun of me was Bih-Ngum.

On one fateful day, my best friend Mambo was scheduled to fight Bih-Ngum after school, but when it was time to go for the scheduled fight, my best friend decided to back out! I was very disappointed and shocked because my best friend had won all her previous fights and the young girl she had to fight did not look as powerful as those my friend had beaten in the past.

Very frustrated with her decision to back out of this fight and having the whole crowd yell "Oho Shame! Oho Shame!" I pulled my friend away to get to the root of the matter. Mambo then confided in me that she had no underwear! I thought about a solution fast and decided to quickly run with her into the bushes remove my own underwear and let her borrow it to wear and proceed with the fight. She wore the underwear, ran out of the bushes and proceeded with the fight. She won the fight in less than no time and I was so happy I asked her to keep the cotton underwear, which was one of only three I owned. Bih-Ngum was humbled after the fight and never messed with me or my best friend ever again.

However, when my gracious Mama heard about the fight and the less than gracious part, I played in it, I was in more trouble than I could have possibly imagined. I was grounded and had to fill two big pots with fresh water from the stream for the rest of that month in addition to my other assigned chores. My luminary Mama told me a few things that I will never forget:

1. God is clear that Christians should not be fist fighting or re-paying evil of any kind.
2. No matter how hard it may seem, if someone slaps you on the cheek, you must turn away from that person.
3. Encouraging friends to fight is worse than engaging in the fight.
4. True friends stand up for you and make sure you stay safe.
5. A loyal friend is not a friend that encourages you to physically fight.
6. Fighting can damage your eyes, teeth or even your internal organs.
7. Walking away from a fight is a sign of strength, not weakness.
8. You can kill someone or be killed in a physical fight.

The first and last lessons scared me so bad I made a promise to myself not only to stay out of physical fights, but also to help others stay out of physical fights as well. Thanks again, Mama! May your gracious soul continue to rest in peace. Amen!

What the Holy Bible says about ancestral wisdom

- **Job 12:12** - Is not wisdom found among the aged? Does not long-life bring understanding?

- **Proverbs 1:8-9** - Listen, my son, to your father's instruction and do not forsake your mother's teaching. They are a garland to grace your head and a chain to adorn your neck.

- **Proverbs 2:11-12** - Discretion will protect you, and understanding will guard you. Wisdom will save you from the ways of wicked men, from men whose words are perverse.

- **Proverbs 3:13-15** - Blessed are those who find wisdom, those who gain understanding, for she is more profitable than silver and yields better returns than gold. She is more precious than rubies; nothing you desire can compare with her.

- **Proverbs 3:21-23** - My son, do not let wisdom and understanding out of your sight, preserve sound judgment and discretion; they will be life for you, an ornament to grace your neck. Then you will go on your way in safety, and your foot will not stumble.

CHAPTER SIX
WISDOM IS NOT HIDDEN

Grandpa Tanyi Mbah's fireside nights of wisdom were always something to write home about! Grandpa always started his evening wisdom talks with the neighborhood kids with one proverb: "If a child washes his hands really clean, he can eat from the same bowl with the elders. While eating, if he shuts his mouth and opens his ears and mind, he can learn a thing or two." The village neighborhood kids heard this proverb so often that they will all echo it as soon as Grandpa Tanyi started the first few words.

Every fireside talk about wisdom was intriguing! One evening, Fonchi defied all signs from his friends not to offend Grandpa and get the whole group in trouble. He dared to ask a question, "Grandpa, can a little boy like me acquire the wisdom of the elders?" Grandpa smiled, congratulated Fonchi for his courage, to the dismay of the other kids. He said, "My son, wisdom is freely accessible, inescapable at the marketplace, and can be found all around you. Thus, go through life with open eyes, ears and mind."

Grandpa always ended his wisdom fireside night talks with "My future wise elders, go through life with eyes of wisdom, ears of wisdom, lips of wisdom, hearts of wisdom and steps of wisdom." Today, more than 30 years after listening to the last wisdom talk of Grandpa Tanyi, I have come to realize that not only was my Grandpa very wise and full of integrity, the Holy Bible confirms his ideas:

> *"Does not wisdom call out? Does not understanding raise her voice? At the highest point along the way, where the paths meet, she takes her stand; beside the gate leading into the city, at the entrance, she cries aloud:"* (Proverbs 8:1-3)

What the Holy Bible says about ancestral wisdom

- **Job 12:12 -** Is not wisdom found among the aged? Does not long-life bring understanding?

- **Proverbs 1:8-9 -** Listen, my son, to your father's instruction and do not forsake your mother's teaching. They are a garland to grace your head and a chain to adorn your neck.

- **Proverbs 2:11-12 -** Discretion will protect you, and understanding will guard you. Wisdom will save you from the ways of wicked men, from men whose words are perverse.

- **Proverbs 3:13-15 -** Blessed are those who find wisdom, those who gain understanding, for she is more profitable than silver and yields better returns than gold. She is more precious than rubies; nothing you desire can compare with her.

- **Proverbs 3:21-23 -** My son, do not let wisdom and understanding out of your sight, preserve sound judgment and discretion; they will be life for you, an ornament to grace your neck. Then you will go on your way in safety, and your foot will not stumble.

CHAPTER SEVEN
YOU MUST DIG YOUR WELL BEFORE YOU GET THIRSTY

Grandma Nimubi always told many tales on our nearly ten-mile walk to the farm, especially during the summer holidays when many of us grandchildren where out of school. Of the many stories she told in many versions, one story she told one rainy morning has stuck on my mind more than all the other hundreds of stories I heard over and over for nearly 10 years. As always, Grandma Nimubi will always start a story with one of the village proverbs: "Make sure you dig your well before you get thirsty."

There was an old man who lived in the village. He was a loner, had two dogs, had no friends, and was very mean to the neighbors. One day, he fell off a tree and shouted for help, but no one came. He eventually died and was buried by the villagers. Grandma explained that this story focuses on the well of life. Water is used because it's life's necessity. Grandma gave a few examples of how to dig your well:

1. Start digging your well by being kind to everyone.
2. Make good friends before you ever need their help.
3. Feed a few people before you ever need to be fed.
4. Go to a few funerals before you ever have one in your compound.
5. Pray against sickness before you ever get sick.

Digging your well before you get thirsty will help you deal with life's issues with diligence.

What the Holy Bible says about planning for the future

- **Proverbs 3:5-6 -** Trust in the Lord with all your heart and lean not on your own understanding; in all your ways submit to Him, and He will make your paths straight.

- **Proverbs 16:3 -** Commit to the Lord whatever you do, and He will establish your plans.

- **Proverbs 16:9 -** In their hearts, humans plan their course, but the Lord establishes their steps.

- **Proverbs 21:5 -** The plans of the diligent lead to profit as surely as haste leads to poverty.

- **Luke 14:28 -** Suppose one of you wants to build a tower. Won't you first sit down and estimate the cost to see if you have enough money to complete it?

CHAPTER EIGHT
OTHER PEOPLE ARE MORE IMPORTANT THAN YOU

Grandma Mandah did not talk much, but when it came to life lessons, she was a champion of hope. On our way to church one Sunday, she decided to lecture on respect and the importance of other people.

1. In everything you do, put God first.
2. You came into the world through other people (father and mother).
3. Other people were your eyes, mouth, and ears before you knew how to use your own eyes and ears.
4. Your life totally depended on other people until you were able to contribute to your own security.
5. Other people will help you along the way to realize your Godly ordained purpose.
6. You are only a true great person because other people say you are.
7. When you die, others will carry your coffin to the grave.

What the Holy Bible says about the importance of others in your life

- **Matthew 6:33 -** But seek first His kingdom and His righteousness, and all these things will be given to you as well.

⚔ **Matthew 7:12 -** So, in everything, do to others what you would have them do to you, for this sums up the Law and the Prophets.

⚔ **Matthew 10:37 -** Anyone who loves their father or mother more than Me is not worthy of Me; anyone who loves their son or daughter more than Me is not worthy of Me.

⚔ **Exodus 20:12 -** Honor your father and your mother, so that you may live long in the land the Lord your God is giving you.

⚔ **Mark 10:44-45 -** And whoever wants to be first must be slave of all. For even the Son of Man did not come to be served, but to serve, and to give His life as a ransom for many.

34

CHAPTER NINE
INTELLIGENCE IS BETTER THAN POWER

Nkweleh? Lehnkwa! Every now and then, we the neighborhood kids had to go through the torture of listening to Papa Ndi Zamu's Mr. Tortoise story and the same questions were asked after the narration, but he would not accept the same answer. It was frustrating to get the answer right one day and give the same answer next time but get in real trouble. He would also yell, "Use your brains! Make good use of your brains! There are always many right answers to one question!" I did not get it then, but I do understand Papa Ndi Zamu's frustrations now as an educated adult. Here goes the famous Mr. Tortoise Story, as told by Papa Ndi Zamu:

Once upon a time, Mr. Tortoise told Mr. Antelope that he can run faster than the latter. This was tantalizing and surprisingly unbelievable to Mr. Antelope, who took it as a joke. And considered it impossible. He, thereupon, advised Mr. Tortoise to propose a date for the said race. So, he did. The conditions for the outcome of the race were that, if Mr Tortoise wins, he would chisel out and own the right horn of the Antelope. Conversely, the tortoise was to lose its shell. Mr. Tortoise, being very shrewd, designed a plan. He had earlier positioned five tortoises on control locations prior to D-day. The fifth tortoise was at the finish line of the track. These arrangements were done behind Mr. Antelope.

He firmly believed that nothing on earth can make Mr. Tortoise win the race, even in hell. Foolish him. The race kicked off. The tortoise was running at a snail's pace, but at each strategic point, when Mr. Antelope calls "Mbelevenleya", a tortoise hidden in the bushes will answer. Mr. Antelope continued running, though distraught, with hidden tortoises answering at every cardinal point of the official track. By the time Mr. Antelope arrived, the winning point of the race, the fifth tortoise had jumped from the bush and already lying on the finish line.

Mr. Tortoise has won. Mr Antelope, heretofore, conceded defeat. He didn't know that this was not the same tortoise with whom he had started the race, since all the tortoises looked alike. He surrendered his right horn to Mr. Tortoise who blew it with unprecedented excitement and mood. Lesson or thematic consideration: "Ezheh e tsah mehteneh", which means "intelligence is better than power".

What the Holy Bible says about ancestral wisdom

- **Job 12:12** - Is not wisdom found among the aged? Does not long-life bring understanding?

- **Proverbs 1:8-9** - Listen, my son, to your father's instruction and do not forsake your mother's teaching. They are a garland to grace your head and a chain to adorn your neck.

- **Proverbs 2:11-12** - Discretion will protect you, and understanding will guard you. Wisdom will save you from the ways of wicked men, from men whose words are perverse.

- **Proverbs 3:13-15** - Blessed are those who find wisdom, those who gain understanding, for she is more profitable than silver and yields better returns than gold. She is more precious than rubies; nothing you desire can compare with her.

- **Proverbs 3:21-23** - My son, do not let wisdom and understanding out of your sight, preserve sound judgment and discretion; they will be life for you, an ornament to grace your neck. Then you will go on your way in safety, and your foot will not stumble.

CHAPTER TEN
TRACE YOUR LINEAGE TO COMPLETE YOUR FAMILY TREE

My ancestors came from four different villages in Cameroon near the West Coast of Central Africa. I remember the night my grandmother told us how she found herself in Akum village, far away from Kom, her village of birth. Her story about her lineage was very sad with many twists and turns but, at the same time, very intriguing. About nine of us gathered around the fireside in my mother's kitchen very eager to hear all about it. This moment was crowned by the eating of some roasted corn and drinking of some warm lemon grass tea (AKA, fever grass tea).

As recounted by my maternal grandmother, her mother was married to a prince of the Kom kingdom. Per the native laws and customs of the Kom people, my mother's grandfather — my great-grandfather — was the next in line to becoming the king of Kom village upon the passing away of his father, the King. His brother who was second in line, allegedly plotted my great-grandfather's death so he could become the next king.

Upon the assassination of my great-grandfather, my great-grandmother, who was then very young feared for her life and the life of her daughter who was just a few months old. They were both smuggled overnight by other members of the royal family into another village called Awing. Had she not escaped, she would have been forced to marry her slain husband's brother; if she refused, she would have been exiled. My great-grandmother was not ready for either one of those possibilities, so she had to act fast. In a strange village not knowing anyone, she had to make new friends and embrace a new family while laying low and not divulging who she really was. Her kindness and humility soon caught the attention of one of the wealthy farmers in that village and he married her.

According to my grandmother, my great-grandmother got married more for protection than love because she mourned her slain husband for as long as my grandmother could remember. Under the protection and parenthood of her new husband, the little girl grew up to be my grandmother and in her second marriage, she had another son. My grandmother loved and respected her stepdad and remembered him as a hardworking, loving and kindhearted man, a great husband, and an amazing father to all his children. My grandmother grew up in the Awing village and when she was a teenager, a trader from Akum village that came often to Awing for business took an interest in her. They got married and they relocated to Akum. She was one of several wives and gave birth to five children. My sweet mother was the middle child.

My grandmother always told us that someday, we will trace her lineage and go back to Kom where a crown will be waiting for us. Unfortunately, neither my great grandmother nor my grandmother ever took the risk to go back to the Kom village. The memories and fear of the unknown kept my great-grandmother and my grandmother away from the rest of the family in Kom until they both died and were buried in Awing and Akum, respectively.

Twenty years after my grandmother passed away, we did some research and my mum, her sister, and a few other family members made the long-awaited trip to the palace of Kom village in the North West Region of Cameroon. Just like my grandmother had told us, the crown of the missing Kom princess was finally placed on my mother's head. She was given gifts that had been kept over the years for my grandmother. The whole group that accompanied my mother to the palace received a royal treatment and the rest of the family members were introduced to the royal family of Kom. The family connection and bond has stayed strong to this day. My mother came back from Kom with a few tips on the importance of tracing your roots:

1. She felt fulfilled knowing she had completed that part of the family tree, as instructed by my late grandmother.
2. She had finally restored her mother's family name and connected to people who shared the same blood as herself.
3. She finally claimed what rightfully belonged to her mother, proving that although your crown may be delayed, it has not been denied.
4. She confirmed that tracing her roots was both inspirational and gave her additional insights about herself. She even noticed tendencies from other royals that were not much different from hers.

When my Mum passed away in 2004, the Kom royal traditional dance accompanied her casket into the church. It was the most beautiful and breathtaking procession I have ever seen. It was gracious and healing! It was simply heavenly! Hundreds of family members from the Kom palace were present at my mother's funeral to pay their last respects.

Thanks to my Kom royal lineage. Thanks to my Kom royal grandmother. May the souls of my Kom ancestors rest in peace. Amen!

What the Holy Bible says about the genealogy of Jesus Christ

- **Matthew 1:1-17:** This is the genealogy of Jesus the Messiah the son of David, the son of Abraham: Abraham was the father of Isaac, Isaac the father of Jacob, Jacob the father of Judah and his brothers, Judah the father of Perez and Zerah, whose mother was Tamar, Perez the father of Hezron, Hezron the father of Ram, Ram the father of Amminadab, Amminadab the father of Nahshon, Nahshon the father of Salmon, Salmon the father of Boaz, whose mother was Rahab, Boaz the father of Obed, whose mother was Ruth, Obed the father of Jesse, and Jesse the father of King David, David was the father of Solomon, whose mother had been Uriah's wife, Solomon the father of Rehoboam, Rehoboam the father of Abijah, Abijah the father of Asa, Asa the father of Jehoshaphat, Jehoshaphat the father of Jehoram, Jehoram the father of Uzziah, Uzziah the father of Jotham, Jotham the father of Ahaz, Ahaz the father of Hezekiah, Hezekiah the father of Manasseh, Manasseh the father of Amon, Amon the father of Josiah, and Josiah the father of Jeconiah and his brothers at the time of the exile to Babylon. After the exile to Babylon: Jeconiah was the father of Shealtiel, Shealtiel the father of Zerubbabel, Zerubbabel the father of Abihud, Abihud the father of Eliakim, Eliakim the father of Azor, Azor the father of Zadok, Zadok the father of Akim, Akim the father of Elihud, Elihud the father of Eleazar, Eleazar the father of Matthan, Matthan the father of Jacob, and Jacob the father of Joseph, the husband of Mary, and Mary was the mother of Jesus who is called the Messiah.

Thus, there were fourteen generations in all from Abraham to David, fourteen from David to the exile to Babylon, and fourteen from the exile to the Messiah.

CHAPTER ELEVEN
THE VILLAGE STORY WITH THREE TITLES

Storytelling is a vital part of the African culture and growing up in the Akum village on the West Coast of Central Africa was a cherished childhood full of stories. One story comes to mind very often because the title varied, depending on who was telling the story. When my Grand aunty who couldn't have any children of her own told the story, it was titled "Blessed to Be Barren". When Grandpa told the story, it was titled "The stone that the builder rejects will become the cornerstone". When Grandma told this same story, she titled it "Treat every child as yours because you don't know who your walking stick will be when you get old". This story with three different titles intrigued me as a little girl and still excites me when I think about it. Here is how it goes:

Once upon a time in a neighboring village up in the mountains, there lived a family of five: Mama Wuli and four daughters. Three of the daughters (Wuliwuli, Wulimami, Mamimitango) were her biological daughters and one, Akwakakwaka, was her stepdaughter. Her husband, Papa Wuli, had two wives and he passed away when the second wife was pregnant with her first child.

A few months after the death of Papa Wuli, his second wife Lum gave birth to a baby girl and named her Akwakakwaka (meaning, trash). She was so depressed after the passing of her husband who was known as the best hunter in the village. Her husband had gotten married to her because Mama Wuli was bringing forth girls only and Lum was from a family that made more boys than girls. Papa Wuli desperately needed a son.

When Papa Wuli died from a poisonous snake bite, the entire village was devastated. He was great with animals and could catch any snake with his bare hands. When Lum gave birth to another baby girl, she was so devastated that she composed a song thanking God sarcastically for not allowing his dear husband to live and see another disappointment. She sang that three disappointments were enough to invite a snake to take away her poor husband's life.

When Akwakakwaka was just five years old, her mother Mama Lum died suddenly after complaining of chest pain. Akwakakwaka was now at the mercy of her stepmother who had developed serious hatred for her and Mama Lum due to her songs that were popular in the village belittling her and her three daughters. Mama Wuli treated her three daughters like princesses and made sure Akwakakwaka was treated more like a maid to her three daughters.

When Akwakakwaka became too filthy and her body filled with wounds, her stepmother decided to isolate her from her three stepsisters. She was put in a little cage and fed with leftovers from the three princesses. One unfortunate day, while Mama Wuli was out to visit her mother about fifteen miles away, a strange animal showed up by the farmhouse, sang a song just like Mama Wuli would sing upon her return. The three princesses ran outside their fenced farmhouse to welcome their mother, but the strange and vicious creature killed all three sisters and disappeared into the forest.

When Mama Wuli got back that night and realized what had happened, she screamed so hard her voice echoed into the village. People came running up the hill to see what had happened to the great hunter's daughters. The village was in mourning. Akwakakwaka was rescued from isolation by one of the village elderly women and when she wanted to take Akwakakwaka away, Mama Wuli begged with every little breath she had left to repent, forgive, and take care of Akwakakwaka as if she was her own very daughter.

She was given the opportunity to keep Akwakakwaka on condition that she will take her wherever she went. She accepted, cleaned Akwakakwaka's wounds, fed her well, made beautiful dresses for her and she soon became the village beauty queen. Her stepmother changed her name from Akwakakwaka (trash) to Eboghn (meaning, blessing). She ended up marrying a handsome hardworking carpenter from a neighboring village.

She took her stepmother with her and cared for her until she died at the age of more than one hundred. Akwakakwaka, now called Eboghn, and her husband were blessed with ten healthy children: seven boys and three girls. She named her three daughters after her three stepsisters.

What the Holy Bible says about ancestral wisdom

- **Job 12:12 -** Is not wisdom found among the aged? Does not long-life bring understanding?

- **Proverbs 1:8-9 -** Listen, my son, to your father's instruction and do not forsake your mother's teaching. They are a garland to grace your head and a chain to adorn your neck.

- **Proverbs 2:11-12 -** Discretion will protect you, and understanding will guard you. Wisdom will save you from the ways of wicked men, from men whose words are perverse.

- **Proverbs 3:13-15 -** Blessed are those who find wisdom, those who gain understanding, for she is more profitable than silver and yields better returns than gold. She is more precious than rubies; nothing you desire can compare with her.

- **Proverbs 3:21-23 -** My son, do not let wisdom and understanding out of your sight, preserve sound judgment and discretion; they will be life for you, an ornament to grace your neck. Then you will go on your way in safety, and your foot will not stumble.

CHAPTER TWELVE
I WAS A SECOND WORLD WAR VETERAN

Grandpa Mufor-Ngu fought in the Second World War and his heroic acts made him a village hero until his death at the age of 102 years old. As recounted by grandpa Mufor-Ngu, growing up as a little boy in the Akum village, he was well liked and greatly admired and respected by many people in the village both young and old. He recalls the horrors of the second world war and his role during the war. His service in the Second World War and the great generals he fought alongside with such as General Sambang, Captain Wakende, and many others. He said even though he was hired to fight on the side of the Germans, he ended the war as a British soldier because of his bravery and ability to swim across the Atlantic Ocean and save other soldiers.

Young boys from the neighboring compounds would come over to my grandpa's house, sit around the fireside and listen to these amazing war stories and how fighting in the war taught him courage, perseverance, wisdom, kindness, integrity, and the ability to cultivate friendships. Grandpa even learned how to speak German while fighting in the Second World War. His heroic stories gave most of us listening to him then, an extra set of wings to fly, and we have been soaring beyond horizons. Grandpa was one of the wisest men I was blessed to sort wisdom from whenever the opportunity presented itself. But most of his heroic stories were not confirmed by my luminary Papa and neither did my Papa discredit these stories. As much wisdom as I got from Grandpa Mufor-Ngu, something in my heart kept questioning some of his stories. Since it was against the native laws and customs of the Akum people to doubt or even question the honesty of an elder, I let it lie for so many years.

When Grandpa Mufor-Ngu turned 100 years old, I was then in college and had mastered the art of interrogation without disrespecting and gathered momentum to ask him about the school he went to with his friends and the subjects that were being taught back then. He smiled, looked at me straight in the face, placed his right hand on my shoulders and whispered, "Every man was created with his own school within him and if you cannot be at the top of your class, then you are not your father's son."

May the soul of Grand Pa. Mufor- Ngu continue to rest in peace!

What the Holy Bible says about ancestral wisdom

- **Job 12:12** - Is not wisdom found among the aged? Does not long-life bring understanding?

- **Proverbs 1:8-9** - Listen, my son, to your father's instruction and do not forsake your mother's teaching. They are a garland to grace your head and a chain to adorn your neck.

- **Proverbs 2:11-12** - Discretion will protect you, and understanding will guard you. Wisdom will save you from the ways of wicked men, from men whose words are perverse.

- **Proverbs 3:13-15** - Blessed are those who find wisdom, those who gain understanding, for she is more profitable than silver and yields better returns than gold. She is more precious than rubies; nothing you desire can compare with her.

- **Proverbs 3:21-23** - My son, do not let wisdom and understanding out of your sight, preserve sound judgment and discretion; they will be life for you, an ornament to grace your neck. Then you will go on your way in safety, and your foot will not stumble.

49

CHAPTER THIRTEEN
GO WHERE YOU ARE CELEBRATED, NOT TOLERATED

Growing up in the Akum village in Cameroon, I looked up to the nuns at the village health center and convent with a lot of admiration. I always wanted to be like them, serve like them, and go to heaven like them when the time was ripe. I prayed to Jehovah God constantly for an opportunity to attend the prestigious Our Lady of Lourdes College, an all-female five-year Catholic secondary school championed mostly by nuns from all over the world.

My wish was granted many years later when at the age of twelve, I was admitted into this prestigious institution. I cannot forget my excitement when I moved into the Bernadette dormitory and settled with the other newcomers from all over the country. The journey I was about to start did not go as I had imagined. My parents worked so hard to keep me in this prestigious school. I came to a quick and shocking realization that the nuns were not angels and could tell lies, discriminate, and be human. They also were quick to make me realize I was not nun material. I would fidget during prayers, eat under my blanket during siesta, speak my mind to the nun when I noticed discrimination, and chew gum in church.

On the bright side, I was able to watch my very first movie at the age of 12 in this prestigious school. The movie was *The Sound of Music*. I totally loved it and could not wait to get home during the Christmas break and share the great movie with my parents and siblings. When I got home for Christmas after three months of being in this prestigious school, I could not wait to defend the comments on my report card and tell my family that the nuns were humans with a lot of faults, too.

Failing to justify the comments in my report card after several attempts, I gave up and told them about *The Sound of Music*. Everyone listened with excitement and at the end of my review of this great movie, my luminary father had a few words for me, "My dear daughter, just like Maria, you will be a problem in the convent and not a solution. You will make God proud someday, but not as a nun. Go where you will be celebrated, not where you will be tolerated." He concluded by lifting his hands to the sky saying, "Father God, I pray you keep me long enough to see what my daughter will be in future." May my luminary Papa's soul continue to rest in peace!

What the Holy Bible says about ancestral wisdom

- **Job 12:12 -** Is not wisdom found among the aged? Does not long-life bring understanding?

- **Proverbs 1:8-9 -** Listen, my son, to your father's instruction and do not forsake your mother's teaching. They are a garland to grace your head and a chain to adorn your neck.

- **Proverbs 2:11-12 -** Discretion will protect you, and understanding will guard you. Wisdom will save you from the ways of wicked men, from men whose words are perverse

- **Proverbs 3:13-15 -** Blessed are those who find wisdom, those who gain understanding, for she is more profitable than silver and yields better returns than gold. She is more precious than rubies; nothing you desire can compare with her.

- **Proverbs 3:21-23 -** My son, do not let wisdom and understanding out of your sight, preserve sound judgment and discretion; they will be life for you, an ornament to grace your neck. Then you will go on your way in safety, and your foot will not stumble.

CHAPTER FOURTEEN
THE IMPORTANCE OF
TIME AND OPPORTUNITY

My luminary late father, Papa Joseph Nkwenti Asafor, was a time-conscious man with many inspiring stories to tell us children about the importance of time and opportunity management. He was a father, teacher, politician, philanthropist, and well-respected member of the community. I cannot thank Jehovah God enough for blessing my family with a wise and loving father like my luminary Papa. He held a voluntary position as president of our village Welfare Association for ten years.

Papa Joseph Nkwenti Asafor will always be remembered by many who were blessed to cross paths with him as a man of integrity and wisdom. His wisdom he shared so generously, his dedication and guidance gave so many people the wings to fly. He believed and inspired many others to acknowledge that true greatness does not only lie in what one has accomplished for oneself, but mostly in what one has inspired others to accomplish for themselves.

Papa believed and encouraged others to seek first the kingdom of God and His righteousness, so that all other things can be accomplished accordingly. Amongst all his teachings, the teachings on time and opportunity were frequent and he not only taught effective time management but also lived what he preached. Below is a list of some of his time and opportunity management teachings:

1. Time management is life management.
2. Time flies, and you are the pilot.
3. Use your time wisely because time waits for no one.

4. Time is priceless and limited.
5. Time is more valuable than money.
6. Time lost can never be recovered.
7. Don't waste time. Make beneficial use of time.
8. Don't give anyone or anything permission to waste your time.
9. Time is free but costly.
10. You can't own time, but you can spend it.
11. Do not postpone until tomorrow things that could be done today.
12. Opportunity comes but once.
13. An opportunity of a lifetime must be seized during the lifetime of that opportunity.
14. Opportunities are like doors: they open and close.

My luminary Papa reminded us always that no matter how brave, swift, old, rich, and wise you are, time and opportunity will affect you negatively if you don't learn how to respond to these two things diligently and promptly.

What the Holy Bible says about time and opportunity

- **Ecclesiastes 9:11** - "I have seen something else under the sun: The race is not to the swift or the battle to the strong, nor does food come to the wise or wealth to the brilliant or favor to the learned; but time and chance happen to them all."

CHAPTER FIFTEEN
LESSONS FROM THE CATERPILLAR

When we were growing up in the Akum village, our parents had a large farm with all varieties of plants, from coffee trees, mango trees, pear trees, guava trees, sugar cane, pawpaw trees to name a few. As kids, we played in the farm, climbed trees, harvested fruits and famously played hide-and-seek. There were also many animals, insects and flies that found comfort in our large farm. I was very scared of snakes and bees.

I detested the caterpillar because it was so sluggish, ugly and whenever it crept on me, my whole body quivered. I loved the butterfly with all my heart and will spend a lot of time running after them in admiration. They were so beautiful and flew so majestically around the farm, beautifying every leaf they landed on. I will dream about butterflies all the time.

One good morning during the coffee picking season, we were in the farm with our luminary Papa picking the red and purple ripe coffee beans amongst the green unripe ones. Suddenly, I felt a cold soft movement on my left elbow and my body quivered and went down my spine. I shouted, knocked off the ugly caterpillar from my elbow, and ran off. When I calmed down and returned to join the rest of the family, I did not find it funny that they were all laughing at what had just happened to me. My Papa told me in the sweetest voice possible, "Daughter of mine, you cannot hate the caterpillar and love the butterfly."

I was seven years old and until that morning, I didn't even know the two were related. When my luminary Papa told me a caterpillar was a butterfly in the making, I was intrigued and secretly vowed to disprove him. I asked Papa over and over how in the world something that long, squishy, and ugly can turn out so beautiful and graceful. Papa answered my question by saying:

1. With God everything is possible.
2. Like the caterpillar, time and chance can turn something ugly into something beautiful.
3. The caterpillar goes through a process of nourishing itself for its future beautiful form as a butterfly.
4. The caterpillar sheds its old skin several times before becoming a butterfly.

After listening to my luminary Papa's explanation of the relationship between the caterpillar and the butterfly, my only concern was that my elbow should never have been part of the process. From that day forward, I stopped hating the caterpillar. Instead I started praying for a smooth transition from egg to butterfly.

One warm summer when I was nine years old, my Papa made me experience the process from egg to caterpillar then to butterfly. It took the egg eight days to turn into the larva/caterpillar and pupa/chrysalis each took twelve days. The final product after one month was a beautiful, graceful butterfly. I named it "Sunshine" and watched it fly away with such beauty and grace.

Thanks to my luminary Papa. May his soul continue to rest in peace!

What the Holy Bible says about ancestral wisdom

- **Job 12:12** - Is not wisdom found among the aged? Does not long-life bring understanding?

- **Proverbs 1:8-9** - Listen, my son, to your father's instruction and do not forsake your mother's teaching. They are a garland to grace your head and a chain to adorn your neck.

▲ **Proverbs 2:11-12** - Discretion will protect you, and understanding will guard you. Wisdom will save you from the ways of wicked men, from men whose words are perverse.

▲ **Proverbs 3:13-15 -** Blessed are those who find wisdom, those who gain understanding, for she is more profitable than silver and yields better returns than gold. She is more precious than rubies; nothing you desire can compare with her.

▲ **Proverbs 3:21-23 -** My son, do not let wisdom and understanding out of your sight, preserve sound judgment and discretion; they will be life for you, an ornament to grace your neck. Then you will go on your way in safety, and your foot will not stumble.

CHAPTER SIXTEEN
LET DOGS DELIGHT TO BARK AND BITE

Once upon a time in St. Julius Primary School in Akum, there existed a luminary teacher named Pa. Ticha Fru. He had zero tolerance for pupils fighting amongst themselves or stealing from each other. Whenever a case of theft or fighting was brought to his attention, those involved will be punished and the rest of the class will be asked to sing a notorious song with the following lyrics starting with your class identification:

Class six is a notorious class.

We fight and steal and play.

We disobey and will not learn and waste our precious time.

On one fateful Wednesday afternoon, the girls were competing against the boys in track. A riot broke out after some of the boys took off running before the whistle was blown to signal the beginning of the race. They got to the finish line first and declared victorious! The girls were furious and decided to settle the score with a fist fight. This quickly got out of control and punches were exchanged left and right. Pa. Ticha Fru and the five other schoolteachers had to use water from school drums to bring the fighting to an end.

With the fighters all wet and frustrated, the least they expected was a request to learn a new song and march to its tune around the school five times before being dismissed for the day. The new song's lyrics were:

Let dogs delight to bark and bite for God has made them so.

Let bears and lions growl and fight for it's their nature, too.

But children, you should never let such angry passions rise,

your little hands were never made to tear each other's eyes.

May the soul of Papa Ticha Fru rest in peace. Amen!

What the Holy Bible says about ancestral wisdom

- **Job 12:12:** Is not wisdom found among the aged? Does not long-life bring understanding?

- **Proverbs 1:8-9:** Listen, my son, to your father's instruction and do not forsake your mother's teaching. They are a garland to grace your head and a chain to adorn your neck.

- **Proverbs 2:11-12**: Discretion will protect you, and understanding will guard you. Wisdom will save you from the ways of wicked men, from men whose words are perverse.

- **Proverbs 3:13-15**: Blessed are those who find wisdom, those who gain understanding, for she is more profitable than silver and yields better returns than gold. She is more precious than rubies; nothing you desire can compare with her.

- **Proverbs 3:21-23**: My son, do not let wisdom and understanding out of your sight, preserve sound judgment and discretion; they will be life for you, an ornament to grace your neck. Then you will go on your way in safety, and your foot will not stumble.

CHAPTER SEVENTEEN
LION AND EAGLE LEADERSHIP ATTITUDE

My Papa was a great leader in his community and greatly respected by his peers and the entire village. He used to tell us repeatedly that he was not the tallest, largest, heaviest, richest or even the most intelligent member of the community. What set him aside from the others was his attitude. He will tell us over and over that "attitude is a small thing that goes a long way". He believed in respecting yourself and others. He lived what he preached.

One Saturday evening during the corn harvesting season, we gathered around the fire getting the corn we had harvested for the last two days ready for drying. Usually, we will use a local method of hanging the bundles of corn on a bamboo stick for months until it was dry enough to take down, grind at the mill for corn flour that was then used for fufu and other local dishes.

On this fateful evening, it started pouring outside and we the kids were granted permission to go play in the rain! We were excited and danced our feet tired and after an hour or so, we were called back in to sit by the fireside and dry off. There was some fresh, sweet, roasted corn and lemongrass tea waiting for us. While we indulged into this delicacy, my brother mentioned that he saw a bunch of eagles fly by earlier that day.

The mention of the eagle triggered a story from my papa about eagles and lions. "Dearest children of mine, do you know that the eagle is the king of the bird kingdom? Do you know that, strangely enough, eagles don't flock? Also, do you know that the lion is the king of the animal kingdom? The eagle is not the fastest, biggest, strongest, nor the smartest bird. Unlike pigeons and other birds who flock together, eagles like real leaders, don't flock. You find them flying alone.

The lion is not the biggest, strongest, fastest or the most intelligent animal. What the eagle and the lion have in common is attitude, I mean leadership attitude! Attitude that commands respect! An attitude that determines the altitude! A decisive attitude! Attitude that inspires others! A positive attitude! An attitude that sets the tone! An attitude that portrays confidence and integrity! So, dearest children of mine, approach life with the attitude of a lion and you will soar beyond horizons like an eagle."

May my luminary Papa's soul continue to rest in peace!

What the Holy Bible says about the lion

- **Proverbs 30:29-30 -** There are three things that are stately in their stride, four that move with stately bearing: a lion, mighty among beasts, who retreats before nothing;

- **Isaiah 31:4 -** This is what the LORD says to me: "As a lion growls, a great lion over its prey and though a whole band of shepherds is called together against it, it is not frightened by their shouts or disturbed by their clamor so the LORD Almighty will come down to do battle on Mount Zion and on its heights."

- **Proverbs 28:1-** The wicked flee though no one pursues, but the righteous are as bold as a lion.

What the Holy Bible says about the eagle

- **Isaiah 40:30-31-** Even youths grow tired and weary, and young men stumble and fall; but those who hope in the LORD will renew their strength. They will soar on wings like eagles; they will run and not grow weary; they will walk and not be faint.

⋏ **Job 39:27-29** - Does the eagle soar at your command and build its nest on high? It dwells on a cliff and stays there at night; a rocky crag is its stronghold. From there, it looks for food; its eyes detect it from afar.

⋏ **Revelation 8:13** - As I watched, I heard an eagle that was flying in midair call out in a loud voice: "Woe! Woe! Woe to the inhabitants of the earth, because of the trumpet blasts about to be sounded by the other three angels!"

CHAPTER EIGHTEEN
LOVING IS GIVING

Growing up with my sweet mother in Akum, she always reminded us that love meant giving away something to another without expecting anything back. It may be yourself, your time, or your resources. She always referred us to John 3:16, "For God so loved the world that He gave His only Son that whoever believes in Him shall not perish but have everlasting life." He showed His love not by what He received, but by what He gave. And how can you ever truly love someone without giving? That's not possible. You can give without loving but unfortunately, you cannot love without giving! Love only grows by sharing!

We do not give because we want praises, we give because it is lovely. It is godly. We give because it is the root source of all blessings. Until you learn to give, you'll never know how to appreciate. Once you start appreciating, then you'll know what it means to give. My sweet mother would always reiterate, "My dear children, as humans we should always give without remembering and receive without forgetting."

May my sweet mother's wise soul continue to rest in peace. Amen!

What the Holy Bible says about loving is giving

- **John 3:16-17-** For God so loved the world that He gave His one and only Son, that whoever believes in Him shall not perish but have eternal life. For God did not send His son into the world to condemn the world, but to save **the** world through Him.

⚠ **Matthew 6:1-4** - "Be careful not to practice your righteousness in front of others to be seen by them. If you do, you will have no reward from your Father in heaven. "So, when you give to the needy, do not announce it with trumpets, as the hypocrites do in the synagogues and on the streets, to be honored by others. Truly I tell you, they have received their reward in full. But when you give to the needy, do not let your left hand know what your right hand is doing, so that your giving may be in secret. Then your Father, who sees what is done in secret, will reward you.

CHAPTER NINETEEN
THE STORY OF THE HUNT WILL ALWAYS GLORIFY THE HUNTER!

Grandpa Mufor was one of the most powerful and respected personalities in our community and even the neighboring villages also knew a thing or two about this great hunter. He went hunting for long hours and brought home more spoils than any of the other hunters in the village. He was a trader in dry bush meat because what he brought home from hunting was more than his family of three wives and 18 children could consume. As little kids growing up, we heard a lot of heroic stories about Grandpa Mufor. We respected and feared him at the same time.

There was an incident where he wrestled with a lion in the forest, killed the lion, and carried it home almost bleeding to death from the wounds inflicted by the vicious animal. The story quickly engulfed the village and his peers came by with some healing herbs and sang songs for the rapid recovery of his "wounds of bravery" as they called it!

When Grandpa's wounds were fully healed, he gathered the children and wives by the fireside for an evening of celebration with some lion meat in vegetable soup made with palm oil, egussi, and yellow fresh hot peppers. Accompanying this delicacy was a big pot of fufu corn cooked to perfection by his second wife Grandma Tigih. The delicious lion meat vegetable soup was prepared by Grandpa Mufor's first wife Grandma Kari.

After the delicious meal was fully consumed, Grandpa told the family the whole story of how the hunt went that day without mentioning his wounds and near-death experience. At the end of the story, he warned the family to hold tight to the following doctrines:

1. The end is what justifies the means!
2. Write your own story; don't leave it in the hands of others who don't even know you.
3. Be your own number one advocate!
4. Don't only preach attitude, demonstrate it as well!
5. Beat your own drum to get others to join you!

May Grandpa Mufor's soul continue to rest in peace. Amen!

What the Holy Bible says about ancestral wisdom

- **Job 12:12** - Is not wisdom found among the aged? Does not long-life bring understanding?

- **Proverbs 1:8-9** - Listen, my son, to your father's instruction and do not forsake your mother's teaching. They are a garland to grace your head and a chain to adorn your neck.

- **Proverbs 2:11-12** - Discretion will protect you, and understanding will guard you. Wisdom will save you from the ways of wicked men, from men whose words are perverse.

- **Proverbs 3:13-15** - Blessed are those who find wisdom, those who gain understanding, for she is more profitable than silver and yields better returns than gold. She is more precious than rubies; nothing you desire can compare with her.

- **Proverbs 3:21-23** - My son, do not let wisdom and understanding out of your sight, preserve sound judgment and discretion; they will be life for you, an ornament to grace your neck. Then you will go on your way in safety, and your foot will not stumble.

CHAPTER TWENTY
IF EVERYONE IS A DRUMMER, THERE WILL BE NO DANCERS AND NO SPECTATORS

Growing up as a little girl in Akum village, we had more ancestors dead and living than any of us kids ever wanted! Some of our ancestors were fun to be around, but some were pure hell on earth, if you ask me! However, when all was said and done, we all realized these ancestors were coming from a good place. They all wanted the best for us and nothing else! How they went about guaranteeing this "best" for us is justified by the popular African proverb "Never bite a finger that fed you." That said, I must share a little about our luminary Grandma Nimungwe.

She told us very often that if everyone played the drum, there will be no one to dance or watch. However, she warned us not to even dare to become spectators or those watching the drummers and the dancers! She threatened that if any of us were related to her, we had to strive to be drummers or, at least, be dancers.

She was very strict, never appreciated anyone's jokes, and had no sense of humor! After being vindicated over and over for not laughing at her jokes, we the neighborhood children decided to laugh out loud whenever she made a joke. Unfortunately for me, one Friday afternoon while assisting her crack egussi for Saturday's pudding, I laughed out very loudly before she even got halfway into telling her joke! Oh boy.

This attitude got the best of Grandma and I was asked to repeat the joke. Of course, I couldn't remember anything she said! She cursed me out repeatedly and even wished that a bird will poop in the middle of my head! The other kids laughed so hard and I was punished to crack an extra cup of egussi after the other kids were dismissed for the day. From that day on, I listened to every boring joke Grandma Nimungwe told and made sure that I only laughed when the others were laughing.

Grandma Nimungwe had a strange way of grouping people. She grouped people into either drummer or dancer or spectator. Drummers were accomplished people with great jobs like doctors, lawyers, teachers, farmers, mothers. Dancers were people such as students, politicians, traders, storekeepers. Spectators were people who had no jobs and were not students or terminally ill or expecting a baby or breastfeeding. Grandma Nimungwe was not a fan of the last group. She had empathy for the old and the sick, but the rest in that group were not her friends.

One summer holiday, our pretty cousin Lumneh met this handsome young man and it was love at first sight! Njilu was a medical student from overseas on holiday in the village! He was brilliant. After completing high school with five Advanced Level Science papers with all A grades, the government gave him a scholarship to study abroad. The whole village celebrated this milestone. Five years after, he was home to look for his bride and my cousin, barely 18 and just out of high school, was the lucky one.

The village kids were all singing about this love story while this handsome man and his family were bracing themselves to visit Grandma Nimungwe. Oops! I didn't tell you my beautiful cousin Lumneh was raised by Grandma Nimungwe after her mum died giving birth to her. Finally, Njilu and his family came to see Grandma Nimungwe to ask Lumneh's hand in marriage. They came bearing gifts and a lot of food. It was an exciting day.

After presenting their request, eating and dancing then followed. After that, Grandma Nimungwe summed up her response to the marriage proposal in the following sentence, "Lumneh is a spectator and you Njilu is a spectator in the white man's land. When you become a drummer, you can come ask for Lum's hand in marriage. Thanks for coming and have a safe trip."

The devastating end to this match made in heaven spread around the village like wildfire and before other girls could dance their way to Njilu's heart, he left for the UK to complete his studies. Unfortunately, Njilu never completed his medical studies to become a doctor.

On the bright side, beautiful Lumneh got over her disappointment by becoming a doctor and got married to a handsome young man he met in medical school. They got Grandma Nimungwe's blessings and got married! They welcomed their first daughter before Grandma Nimungwe passed away at age of 97 years old.

May Grandma Nimungwe's soul continue to rest in peace. Amen!

What the Holy Bible says about ancestral wisdom

- **Job 12:12** - Is not wisdom found among the aged? Does not long-life bring understanding?

- **Proverbs 1:8-9** - Listen, my son, to your father's instruction and do not forsake your mother's teaching. They are a garland to grace your head and a chain to adorn your neck.

- **Proverbs 2:11-12** - Discretion will protect you, and understanding will guard you. Wisdom will save you from the ways of wicked men, from men whose words are perverse.

- **Proverbs 3:13-15** - Blessed are those who find wisdom, those who gain understanding, for she is more profitable than silver and yields better returns than gold. She is more precious than rubies; nothing you desire can compare with her.

- **Proverbs 3:21-23** - My son, do not let wisdom and understanding out of your sight, preserve sound judgment and discretion; they will be life for you, an ornament to grace your neck. Then you will go on your way in safety, and your foot will not stumble.

CHAPTER TWENTY-ONE
LOVE SHOULD NOT BE THE FOUNDATION OF A GODLY MARRIAGE

My luminary Papa and my sweet mother were married for over forty years before my Papa passed away in 1987. My Papa had some serious health problems, but always reminded us that he was also serving a big God. He accomplished way more than ten healthy men combined, if you asked me! I was only 17 years old when my Papa went to be with the Lord and though devastated, I couldn't help but admire what a champion of hope he was for his family and the community. He wore many hats in the village, including teacher, doctor, politician, farmer, marriage counsellor, adviser, and renowned village philanthropist. He shared his time and wisdom so generously and inspired many people, young and old, to dream big and fulfil their Godly ordained purposes on earth.

Our village was mostly made up of happy, hardworking people who believed in not sparing the rod and spoiling the child! The married women stayed married and the married men stayed married. Occasionally, they extended their families by getting married to two or more wives! Fortunately for my family, my father stayed married to just my mother! My father believed and voiced frequently that God created **marriage** as a loyal partnership between one **man** and one woman as the firmest foundation for building a family.

One Christmas holiday, just three years before my Papa went to be with the Lord, Uncle Mbah, my Papa's younger nephew, brought his young wife, Aunty Awa to the village from the economic capital of Douala to come seek advice from my Papa. We were happy to see them, especially since they came bearing gifts for all the children. As inquisitive as I was back then, I succeeded in hiding behind the cupboard to listen to the reason for the visit! Uncle started by telling my father that Aunty Awa was lazy.

Whenever she was given money for food, she will first buy her expensive body lotion and if there was any change left over, she will buy whatever she could, come home, and go to sleep for the rest of the day. He continued by telling my father that he wanted to divorce her or get a second wife who could behave better. Aunty Awa explained that Uncle Mbah was sleeping around with another young woman and was very stingy with money. She said she was not in love with him anymore and wanted out as well. My luminary Papa had the following lessons for Uncle Mbah and Aunty Awa:

1. Mbah, you don't need to divorce Awa, and you don't need a second wife.
2. Awa, love does not make marriage work, and it is not the foundation of marriage.
3. Both of you, listen to me carefully: a successful marriage is a result of the application of knowledge, not the exchange of love.
4. Therefore, you both must understand God's purpose for marriage, understand how to settle disputes, understand that no marriage is irreparable.
5. You both need to show each other tough love, Godly love, unconditional love as you go through the intriguing but tough school of marriage.
   Uncle Mbah and Aunty Awa took my Papa's advice and confessed after my Papa went to be with the Lord that his wise counsel enabled their "irreconcilable differences" to gradually fade away as they constantly learned to seek and apply wisdom to their marriage. They stayed happily married till this day.
   May my luminary Papa's soul continue to rest in peace. Amen!

What the Holy Bible says about love and marriage

- **Genesis 2:22-24** - Then the LORD God made a woman from the rib He had taken out of the man, and He brought her to the man. The man said, "This is now bone of my bones and flesh of my flesh; she shall be called 'woman,' for she was taken out of man." That is why a man leaves his father and mother and is united to his wife, and they become one flesh.

- **1 Corinthians 13:4-7-** Love is patient, love is kind. It does not envy, it does not boast, it is not proud. It does not dishonor others, it is not self-seeking, it is not easily angered, it keeps no record of wrongs. Love does not delight in evil but rejoices with the truth. It always protects, always trusts, always hopes, always perseveres.

- **Ephesians 5:25-29** - Husbands, love your wives, just as Christ loved the church and gave Himself up for her to make her holy, cleansing her by the washing with water through the word, and to present her to Himself as a radiant church, without stain or wrinkle or any other blemish, but holy and blameless. In this same way, husbands ought to love their wives as their own bodies. He who loves his wife loves himself. After all, no one ever hated their own body, but they feed and care for their body, just as Christ does the church.

- **1 John 4:7-11** - Dear friends, let us love one another, for love comes from God. Everyone who loves has been born of God and knows God. Whoever does not love does not know God, because God is love. This is how God showed His love among us: He sent His one and only Son into the world that we might live through him. This is love: not that we loved God, but that He loved us and sent His Son as an atoning sacrifice for our sins. Dear friends, since God so loved us, we also ought to love one another.

➤ **1 John 4:18 -** There is no fear in love. But perfect love drives out fear, because fear has to do with punishment. The one who fears is not made perfect in love.

CHAPTER TWENTY-TWO
THE PURPOSE OF YOUR EXISTENCE

One beautiful summer night in 1979, we all gathered around the dining table in our living room playing one of the family favorite games called "Ludo Snakes and Ladders" with our luminary Papa. We were having so much fun until our neighbor's grandson, Ngwa, pushed open the living room door and ran straight into my father's arms crying!

After getting him to stop crying, my father asked him what the problem was. He started sobbing again and explained that he was tired of being called "mistake" by his young uncles and aunties. It so happened that he had accidentally kicked his auntie's bowl of "cold water garri" into a dirty pile of coco yam peelings. His young aunty, who was just two years older than him, slapped him across the face and called him a destructive mistake.

Ngwa's mother Ateh was just 15 years old when her parents discovered she was about 6 months pregnant by her 16-year-old village sweetheart. Her father gave her a serious beating, watched by the neighborhood kids and all Ateh could get out of her mouth was "It was a mistake" over and over as she received the beating until her mother and two other mothers got her out of her father's sight and took her to seek refuge at her grandma's house. She finally gave birth to Ngwa and made peace with her parents and was brought back home with the baby. The neighborhood kids and even baby Ngwa's own aunties and uncles decided to call him "mistake". This unfortunate name that came from her mother's scream while pregnant stayed as a label on poor Ngwa until my luminary Papa brought an abrupt end to it! After consoling the five-year-old Ngwa and promising anyone who called him "mistake" the punishment of filling 4 drums with clean water from the mile-long stream, Ngwa smiled, and promised to bring the names of any culprit before my father for justice!

When Ngwa two young uncles and one young aunty came to get him from our house, my luminary Papa asked them to sit down and used the opportunity for a teaching moment:

"No human being on earth was created accidentally. No one of us is a mistake! God almighty, the creator of the heavens and the earth, created every one of you for a designed purpose. He put some thought, deep thought into your creation. In order to understand better, you will help me answer these three questions: Who are you? Where did you come from? Why are you here?

Most of the kids shouted that the questions were very simple and easy to answer! I answered the first question: "I am Ngwe, your best daughter." My small cousin Bibi answered the second question: "I came from my mama's belly." My nephew who was visiting from the capital city answered the third question: "I am stubborn, and my mum sent me here to the village so you can teach me a lesson." Papa smiled and said, "Congratulations, future leaders. You answered well, but listen to the remaining part of your answers and never forget the following:

1. Who are you? You are God's specially anointed child created for a divine purpose.
2. Where did you come from? You came to earth from heaven. You came to earth through Mama and Papa. You came to earth through the Akum village in Cameroon near the West Coast of Central Africa.
3. Why am I here? You are here on earth to fulfil a divine purpose.

If you got Question 1 wrong, you will have 2 and 3 wrong. Knowing who you are gives you the wisdom to know who your creator and what mission He has assigned for you here on earth."

What the NIV of the Holy Bible says about who you are, where you came from and why you were created

- **Ephesians 1:11-12** - In Him we were also chosen, having been predestined according to the plan of Him who works out everything in conformity with the purpose of His will, in order that we, who were the first to put our hope in Christ, might be for the praise of His glory (God chose us when He planned creation).

- **Acts 17:28** - For in Him we live and move and have our being. As some of your own poets have said, 'We are His offspring.'

- **Jeremiah 1:4-5** - The word of the LORD came to me, saying, "Before I formed you in the womb, I knew you, before you were born I set you apart; I appointed you as a prophet to the nations."

- **Psalm 139:15-16** - My frame was not hidden from you when I was made in the secret place, when I was woven together in the depths of the earth. Your eyes saw my unformed body; all the days ordained for me were written in your book before one of them came to be.

- **Psalm 139:13** - For You created my inmost being; You knit me together in my mother's womb.

- **Psalm 139:14** - I praise You because I am fearfully and wonderfully made; Your works are wonderful; I know that full well.

- **Jeremiah 29:11** - For I know the plans I have for you," declares the LORD, "plans to prosper you and not to harm you, plans to give you hope and a future.

CHAPTER TWENTY-THREE
AVOIDING A FIGHT IS A MARK OF HONOR

Growing up, our grandparents and parents made it clear to us that as children of the most high God, we should avoid arguing, fist fighting, creating drama, or repaying evil of any kind. We watch them year after year walk away from awkward situations that would have resulted in fist fighting or serious arguing. At least, the good thing with the adults was that when you walked away from a fight or an argument, the others did not make fun of you and label you a chicken! It was much harder for us young kids to do that because some of these young village kids were straight from hell, smelled like hell and looked like hell.

When we explain our vulnerable situation to our parents and grandparents, they would always remind us that no matter how hard it may seem, if someone says some nasty words to you, don't repay them back, walk or run away, if possible. They would also remind us that attacking violence with violence only brings more violence. They would always reiterate "If you cannot talk sense into their head, run for your dignity and dear life! Later, before you go to sleep, do not forget to pray for yourself and pray for those trying to engage you in a fist fight. Always remember to ask God to help you and to help them as well."

This great advice was put into practice and all seemed to be going well until this boy in my class provoked me beyond my limits, no matter how often I ran away from him, he kept pursuing me. He kicked me from behind and I fell face down. When I recovered from the kick and the fall, he was nowhere in sight! I asked around and was told he ran home to his mom. I forgot all I had been taught and ran as fast as I could to the young man's house. As soon as he spotted me, he climbed up into the attic. I quickly climbed up behind him, brought him down, and gave this young man a beating of a lifetime in his own kitchen and in front of his own mother.

When I was done settling the score, I ran back to school and joined the others as if nothing had happened! About half-an-hour later, his mum brought him to school in bad shape to report the matter to my father who was one of the great teachers in my primary school. At first, he was shocked and not very happy with me! He gave me a serious warning and some punishment for fighting and for doing so outside the school premises.

Later that day, I secretly heard him telling my sweet mother how proud he was of me for standing up to the bully! My parents, however, warned me that I should never fist fight again and promised me hell on earth if I did! It was my first and last fight ever. News spread across the village like wildfire and no one messed with me again after that. I became a village "champion of hope" and an advocate for "avoiding a fight as a mark of honor".

May the souls of my parents and grandparents rest in peace. Amen!

What the Holy Bible says about avoiding a fight

- **Proverbs 20:3 -** It is to one's **honor** to avoid strife, but every fool is quick to quarrel.

- **Colossians 3:8 -** But now, put off all such things as anger, rage, malice, slander, abusive language from your mouth.

- **Ephesians 4:31 -** Let all bitterness, wrath, anger, quarreling, and slander be put away from you, along with all hatred.

- **James 4:1** - What causes fights and quarrels among you? Don't they come from your desires that battle within you?

- **Proverbs 24:29** - Don't say, "I'll do to him like he did to me, I'll be sure to pay him back for what he did."

- **Romans 12:17-19** - Don't pay people back with evil for the evil they do to you. Focus your thoughts on those things that are considered noble. As much as it is possible, live in peace with everyone. Don't take revenge, dear friends. Instead, let God's anger take care of it. After all, Scripture says, "I alone have the right to take revenge. I will pay back, says the Lord."

- **Romans 12: 20-21** - But, "If your enemy is hungry, feed him. If he is thirsty, give him a drink. If you do this, you will make him feel guilty and ashamed." Don't let evil conquer you but conquer evil with good.

- **Matthew 5:39** - But I tell you not to oppose an evil person. If someone slaps you on your right cheek, turn your other cheek to him as well.

- **Psalm 37:8** - Refrain from anger and forsake wrath! Fret not yourself; it tends only to evil.

CHAPTER TWENTY-FOUR
A WHITE MAN HAS LANDED ON THE MOON

Growing up in Akum village with a family as mine accorded us the opportunity to learn and grow to become the competent and transformative leaders that we are in the modern-day work force today. As girls and boys younger than 10 years old, the village life was all we knew and cherished. But one summer in 1969 one of our friends, Fru, then nine years old had the chance to travel to the capital city with his uncle and spent two months in Yaounde.

We, the neighborhood kids, couldn't wait for his triumphant return! When he finally came back, the news spread like wildfire and the first night after his return about 20 neighborhood kids gathered in the compound of Fru's father and listened to all the intriguing city stories! Fru shared some biscuits and candy from his trip and even showed us a poster of Michael Jackson! We had heard about this great musician, but it was the first time most kids put a face to the name! With no television in the country then, we had heard his music on the radio. We were thrilled! Fru promised to teach us how to moon dance like Michael Jackson for a small fee! Speaking about moon-dancing, Fru promised us a story the next day that will totally blow our minds! We separated late that night with everyone anxiously looking forward for the great story the next day.

The next evening three more kids from 3 miles away heard about this great story preview and joined us under the moonlight. Fortunately, the night was beautiful, and the moon was shining so bright with a lot of stars in the sky! Fru told all of us to focus on the moon. Then, he announced, "I am here to share the greatest news of all time with you! A White Man in America has landed on the moon, this very moon you are looking at! The story is all over the capital city! His name has not been released yet, but for now he is being referred to as "I am Strong" Oh yes! He was strong indeed!" At this point, every little jaw dropped, and mouths were wide open in shock!

After processing the news, I got up ran to our house, kicked open the living room door, and told my luminary Papa who was using the kerosene lamp to read a newspaper that he needed to come with me and hear for himself! After calming me down and rebuking me for not knocking before entering, he told me he was reading the same moon landing from a newspaper he got from downtown Abakwa earlier that day. He nevertheless decided to walk the half-mile journey with me to Fru's father's compound were the other children were gathered.

When we got there, my luminary Papa greeted Fru's parents. Fru's father brought out two bamboo chairs and some fresh palm wine. The two Papas sat in the middle of these excited kids and asked Fru to repeat the moon landing story! After telling it again, everyone applauded him. It was now time for my Papa to speak! He confirmed Fru's story but added that the man's name has finally been released as "Neil Armstrong". We all applauded Papa! The kids started asking question after question for God alone knows how long it took! My luminary Papa's answers were as follows:

1. Neil Armstrong used the spaceflight Apollo 11 to get to the moon.
2. No, there were no traditional dances waiting to receive Neil Armstrong.
3. No, he did not go with family and friends; he went with Pilot Buzz Aldrin.
4. No, Neil Armstrong is an astronaut.
5. Yes, God made the moon. God made two great lights: the sun to govern the day and the moon to govern the night.
6. Yes, He also made stars.

7. No, there are more than 300 moons in the solar system.

8. Yes, there are nine planets discovered so far: Mercury, Venus, Earth, Mars, Jupiter, Saturn, Uranus, Neptune and Pluto.

9. Yes! We are on the third planet called Earth.

10. Yes! Some planets have more than one moon and others have no moon at all.

11. Mercury and Venus are the only planets that do not have any moon.

12. You are right! Earth has only one moon.

13. Mars has two moons.

14. Jupiter has 79 moons.

15. Saturn has 62 moons

16. Uranus has 27 moons.

17. Neptune has 14 moons.

18. Pluto has 5 moons.

The night ended with Fru becoming a small village hero overnight and my luminary Papa made me proud once more with how much knowledge and wisdom he had yet still very humble and shared his wisdom so generously. Even Fru's father looked at my Papa with awe and admiration. We planned to meet again the next night under the moonlight.

For the next 12 months, we the neighborhood kids would gather in the yard mostly in our compound at night when the moon was out. We sang and watched carefully to see if another person would land on the moon. We watched night after night until Fru travelled to Yaoundé for a second time during the summer holidays and came back with bad news.

After telling us all the wonderful stories about life in the city, he said we may never see anyone land on the moon unless we had a "telescope" which is a very expensive instrument only used by grown-ups. My Papa consoled me by telling me nothing was impossible if you believe and trust God! I promised to get a telescope when I grew up. So was the end of our much-anticipated citing of the second historic moon landing.

May my luminary Papa's soul rest in peace!

What the Holy Bible says about the lunar system

- **Genesis 1:14** - "And God said, let there be lights in the firmament of the heaven to divide the day from the night; and let them be for signs, and for seasons, and for days, and years:"

- **Genesis 1:16** - "God made two great lights—the greater light to govern the day and the lesser light to govern the night. He also made the stars."

- **Psalm 89:37** - "Like the moon, it shall be established forever, a faithful witness in the skies."

- **Psalm 8:3** - "When I look at your heavens, the work of your fingers, the moon and the stars, which You have set in place,"

- **Deuteronomy 4:19** - "And beware lest you raise your eyes to heaven, and when you see the sun and the moon and the stars, all the host of heaven, you be drawn away and bow down to them and serve them, things that the Lord your God has allotted to all the peoples under the whole heaven."

CHAPTER TWENTY-FIVE
LEADERSHIP IS AN ACTION, NOT A POSITION

When I was seven years old, my sweet mother was ill and had to be taken from the village to Douala, the economic capital, to see a specialist. Being the great mother that she was, she insisted on taking me and my baby brother Cho with her! My handsome little brother was about five years old, and just like me, had never travelled out of the village before. We were told the journey will take about five hours in the bus and I spent sleepless nights dreaming what the experience was going to be. We were told about the trip just four days before and warned not to share the news with our host of friends.

We were excited about the journey, but very sad that we couldn't share the great news! After successfully keeping this news a secret for three days, I confided in my best friend Ateh and warned her not to tell anyone! On the morning of our departure, almost every one of our friends showed up that Saturday morning to bid us safe journey! One friend brought three ripe bananas and another friend brought two ripe oranges.

When my Mum got out of the kitchen and saw the nine kids staring at her, she screamed my name and I immediately knew I was dead and buried! She pulled my right ear so hard I thought for a second I had lost the ear. Fortunately, the ear survived, and the five-hour ride was very awkward. I couldn't wait to get to Douala. The journey was very long and uncomfortable, I was dizzy, confused and so sick in the stomach my mother had to give me a plastic bag where I threw up everything, I had eaten that morning. Shortly after I felt sick, my cute little brother felt sick and threw up several times, too. Unfortunately, we couldn't drink the water my Mother carried in her bag because the bus driver had warned that there was no stopping until we get to "Nkemkem", which was the rest area and about halfway between Bamenda and Douala.

When we finally got to "Nkemkem", you could hear the sigh of relief from my mother and other passengers. At this rest place, we were overwhelmed with all the food, drinks and fruits that were being sold there! This place was way bigger than our biggest village market and had more of everything. First, we headed to the restrooms and after that, it was time for lunch. My sweet mother forgot my sin for a moment and asked us to pick whatever we wanted to eat. Oh God! After picking about six items, she changed her mind and said, "Hold on. Pick just two items each, so you don't get sick in the stomach."

I was kind of disappointed but couldn't dare voice it or even show it. I finally picked some roasted ripe plantains and roasted beef (aka soya). My cute brother picked roasted ripe plantain and roasted plums. I shared my soya with him, and he shared his plums with me. We both shared a small bottle of Fanta soda. It was like Christmas in June.

When the driver finished drinking his second bottle of the alcoholic drink Guinness, he announced that it was time to go. Everyone hurried in and those who had not finished eating brought their food on the bus. As soon as we took off, I went to sleep until we got to Douala. When I woke up, I realized my cute baby brother was also sleeping.

When we got out of the bus, my big sister was at the bus stop waiting for us. I had not seen her in over two years. She was very beautiful, smelled so good, already a grown woman and married. She was so happy to see us and after loading the foodstuff we brought from the village, I was so shocked to see that she was the one driving! It was my second time seeing a woman drive a car! The first time was the Reverend Sister in the Village Health Center. I was so proud of my sister and could not wait to go back to the village and tell my friends.

I vowed to drive a car one day when I grow up! A few minutes into the ride home, my sister stopped. Ahead were many cars that were just not moving, so I started playing a car counting game with my baby brother but soon got tired of it because the cars were just not moving. A young boy about my height came towards our car selling cold bottled water. My sister asked him what was happening ahead of us and he said there was an accident. I was frightened and wondered if everyone got out okay! When the cars started moving, we got to the intersection and I noticed a mad man, very dirty with long filthy hair and dressed in rags with no shoes directing traffic. For a second, I thought I was dreaming. Not only am I seeing a mad man in the city, he was working as a policeman!

I thought, "Wonders never end!" I asked my sister why the mad man was directing traffic, she laughed and said, "At least, he helped us go through this junction!" I couldn't wait to go back to the village and share the news with my friends! City life was beginning to be very intriguing and we were not even home at my sister's yet. When we finally got to her house, it was very neat, beautiful, many bedrooms, and even the toilets were in the house! Wonders never end! She introduced us to her house help and her brother-in-law. She had a cute baby called "Daddy" — very adorable. My sister's husband later came home, he was happy to see us, and we had a great dinner.

We slept in this beautiful bedroom with beautiful bed covers. When we got out of bed in the morning, breakfast was ready on the table and we were more than grateful. Later that day, my mother was taken to the specialist. She underwent abdominal surgery and was in the hospital for a few weeks. We stayed with our big sister and her house help took great care of us. The next day, I got into trouble for going to the neighbors' house to invite her kids to come out and play with us. Until then, I thought city life was great, but getting in trouble for going to the neighbor's house was unheard of! That morning, our big sister had a few rules for us:

1. You cannot go visiting neighbors as if you are in the village.
2. You must always wear shoes when you go out of the house.

3. You must use a spoon or fork or teaspoon to eat food like rice, beans, porridge.

We had to wear shoes all the time while outside. No way! Our poor feet suddenly became prisoners of shoes. Eating with utensils, trust me, these utensils can really slow you down. Even though we were not assigned as many chores as we have in the village, we soon realized the village was where we belonged! The village was where the most fun happened! The village was a place where your feet were free!

We respected the city rules and secretly prayed for our mother to recover quickly so we could go back to the fun-filled village life. How could city people live in a house and put a toilet next to the kitchen? I, however, ignored the bad things of the city and enjoyed the good ones like music all over the town and the candy shops next to my sister's house. We even discovered that the same hailstones we collect and eat when there is serious rain in the village could be manmade using the refrigerator and they're called "ice". This ice is then used to make water and soda cooler, especially since Douala was very hot. It was nothing like the cold nice village weather.

Unlike life in the village, it was easy to find coins around the house and my sister's house help will usually let us have it. I will hold my cute baby brother's hand cross the street and go buy candy to save and take to our friends in the village. We missed being knocked down by the reckless Douala drivers quite a few times, but we kept that a secret, too.

Finally, our sweet mother fully recovered from her surgery and it was time to go back home, sweet home! Our big sister bought us some new clothes, underwear, shoes, and school bags. We had a lot of candy, chocolate and biscuits that we bought and saved for our family and friends back home. We also learned a few words, phrases, and even sentences in French, and couldn't wait to show off in the village.

Like everything else, the long journey back home finally came to an end. We got home late in the evening and our luminary Papa was very happy to see us. He had cooked a special meal to welcome us and we all feasted, and he asked us to tell him what we saw and heard in the city! I told them everything and even about the mad man in the city directing traffic. When I was done talking, my luminary Papa said the mad man's story was the most important story we brought back! Really, Papa? Why? He said it was because the madman displayed leadership in action.

He concluded by saying that leadership is an action, not a position, a decision or willingness to lead! He continued by saying that one must take action that inspires people to follow him and that the madman did just that by directing the traffic! Papa concluded that nobody follows anybody who doesn't do anything; people follow people who do something of significance. The madman did just that one significant something!

I then asked him if holding my baby brother's hand and crossing the street was leadership and he said yes! From that day on, I learned that anyone could practice leadership! The next evening, after having so much fun with our friends, I told them all the good and bad stories of city life and concluded with the leadership action of the madman directing traffic. I became a young leadership advocate and vowed to grow up and be a great leader like my Luminary Papa and Sweet Mother.

May their souls continue to rest in peace. Amen!

What the NIV of the Holy Bible says about leadership

- **Galatians 6:9-** Let us not become weary in doing good, for at the proper time we will reap a harvest if we do not give up.

- **Hebrews 13:7-** Remember your leaders, who spoke the word of God to you. Consider the outcome of their way of life and imitate their faith.

⊥ **Isaiah 41:10-** So, do not fear, for I am with you; do not be dismayed, for I am your God. I will strengthen you and help you; I will uphold you with my righteous right hand.

⊥ **James 1:12** -Blessed is the one who perseveres under trial because, having stood the test, that person will receive the crown of life that the LORD has promised to those who love him.

⊥ **1 Peter 5:5** -You younger men, likewise, be subject to your elders; and all of you, clothe yourselves with humility toward one another, for God is opposed to the proud, but gives grace to the humble.

CHAPTER TWENTY-SIX
IF YOU FAIL TO PLAN, YOU PLAN TO FAIL

My sweet mother was not only the matriarch of the Asafor family but a master planner as well. Growing up around her, it was common knowledge that she planned every year from January to December, every month from first day of the month to last day, every week from Sunday to Saturday, and every day from sunrise to sunset. She always concluded her plans with the phrase "by God's grace". She started every day by giving thanks to God and ended it by giving thanks to God. We heard the sentence "If you fail to plan, then plan to fail" too often that we would complete it sometimes, if we thought we could get away it.

Most of our impulsive requests where often met with "Was that planned?" or "Just when did you decide this?" Oh yes, you had to plan almost everything while under my sweet mother's watch! With practice, we gradually became good planners and it really felt good planning and following up on the plans! We will occasionally overhear our sweet mother talk to our luminary Papa about plans five, six and even ten years in advance and will conclude every plan with "by God's grace".

One rainy Wednesday in August, we the kids got excited thinking the almost 9-mile walk to the farm was not going to happen as planned. I secretly prayed it will rain harder, but the more I prayed, the less it rained! And then less than an hour after the rain started pouring down from the sky, it abruptly came to an end. My sweet mother announced, "Children, the rain wasn't in our plan and God's grace has stopped the rain. Get ready, let's head out." Wow! So, even God and the rain were working for my sweet mother and against me! No problem. I decided to plan on having a great day going to the farm with the rest of the family. At the end of that day, I was glad I planned for the best, not the worst. It was an exciting day filled with laughter and memories!

Later that evening by the fireside, I asked my sweet mother why planning was so important. She had a few lessons to teach us on the importance of planning:

1. God the creator is a master planner and is aware of everything because He planned both the beginning and the end.
2. A plan tells you what you want to do and what you don't want to do.
3. As a human, you must plan because humans are the only creatures with the ability to plan.
4. Plans may change but your God-ordained purpose for your life stays the same.
5. Planning your life is crucial because it gives meaning to your time on earth.
6. It is OK to dream but always remember that dreams don't change your life, but plans do.
7. Planning is the key to unlocking your future and whether you succeed or fail in life depends on the plan you have or don't have.

Preparation for realizing God's purpose in your life

Learn to give meaning to your time on earth by planning

Act of faith, firmly believing God's plans to prosper you, give you hope and a future

Now is the time to plan, not later

Never plan without action

Invest in counseling when you plan

Not for heaven, because in heaven, life is eternal

Groundwork for activities between birth and death

May my sweet mother's soul continue to rest in peace. Amen!

What the NIV of the Holy Bible says about planning

- **Proverbs 15:22** - Plans fail for lack of counsel, but with many advisers they succeed.

- **Proverbs 16:3** - Commit to the Lord whatever you do, and He will establish your plans.

- **Jeremiah 29:11** - "For I know the plans I have for you," declares the Lord, "plans to prosper you and not to harm you, plans to give you hope and a future."

- **Proverbs 19:21** - Many are the plans in a person's heart, but it is the LORD's purpose that prevails.

- **Psalm 20:4** - May He give you the desire of your heart and make all your plans succeed.

- **Proverbs 20:18** - Plans are established by seeking advice; so, if you wage war, obtain guidance.

- **Proverbs 21:5** - The plans of the diligent lead surely to abundance, but everyone who is hasty comes only to poverty.

CHAPTER TWENTY-SEVEN
IF YOU THINK EDUCATION IS EXPENSIVE, TRY IGNORANCE

Growing up in a family with five siblings who were girls and two siblings who were boys, it was not unusual to hear family members and friends trying to convince our luminary Papa to only further the education of the boys and not the girls. Though my father was considered one of the smartest and wisest men in the village, some villagers still thought they could voice their opinions on how he should educate or not educate his children! We would often hear the villagers murmur under their breaths how it was a waste of money sending the girl child to secondary school, high school, and university education for a daughter was almost an abomination, according to some of these villagers. They would often discuss over a cup of palm wine and kolanuts how the place of the daughter was in the kitchen and on the farm, not in the classroom.

One evening in 1984, my luminary Papa came home from the Catholic parish office in our village with the news that I had been accepted into the prestigious Our Lady of Lourdes Secondary School Mankon Bamenda, an all-girls boarding secondary school. The whole family was so excited! About 500 young girls had interviewed for this school and I was one of the 85 girls selected to attend. Shortly after this great news, one of our regular visitors Massa Tom (noted for always showing up when my Papa was eating) showed up and joined my Papa for dinner in the family living room. When I went in to give my Papa an extra plate, I overhead him lamenting why my father was working too hard and wasting money on educating women, who will sooner or later become the property of other men. I was aggravated and wished for one second I could tell him a piece of my mind! Unfortunately, I was raised to hold my tongue and most importantly, to respect my elders, including their useless opinions! However, I planned on addressing the issue with my luminary Papa when it was appropriate.

Later that evening, when my sweet mother came back from choir practice and after congratulating me on my admission into Lourdes College, Papa joined us in the kitchen for some teatime by the fireside. My sweet mother had boiled a pot of lemon grass and sweetened it with some natural honey. Accompanying the lemongrass tea was some bread my father had bought from the local market the previous day. It was a beautiful evening and a great time to talk about Massa. Tom's opinion about not educating the daughter. When I asked Papa what business his friend had always meddling into our family meal times and affairs, he had the following advice to give:

1. If you think education is expensive, try ignorance.
2. Educating the girl child is not a waste of money; it is the education of a nation.
3. Every one of my eight children have been given an equal opportunity to education; you are all equally precious to me.
4. You will never be anyone's property; you are a child of the Most High.
5. Ignorance is the cause of all destruction and more expensive than education.
6. Knowledge of the truth is the key to freedom.
7. Massa Tom's opinion should and cannot change your God-ordained potential.

On that note, I decided to once more forgive Massa Tom and his ignorance and look forward to an exciting five years in the prestigious Our Lady of Lourdes College. I made a promise to myself that I was going to be a good girl, make God, my family, and my village proud!

May my luminary Papa's soul continue to rest in peace. Amen!

What the Holy Bible says about lack of knowledge/ignorance

- **Hosea 6:6 -** My people are destroyed from lack of knowledge. Because you have rejected knowledge, I also reject you as my priests; because you have ignored the law of your God, I also will ignore your children.

- **Proverbs 3:5-6 -** Trust in the LORD with all your heart and lean not on your own understanding; in all your ways submit to him, and he will make your paths straight.

- **Ephesians 4:18 -** They are darkened in their understanding and separated from the life of God because of the ignorance that is in them due to the hardening of their hearts.

- **Proverbs 28:26 -** Whoever trusts in his own mind is a fool, but he who walks in wisdom will be delivered.

- **Proverbs 14:15 -** The simple believes everything, but the prudent gives thought to his steps.

CHAPTER TWENTY-EIGHT
YOU CANNOT TEACH WITHOUT LEARNING

My luminary Papa was a well-respected teacher not only in my village but in many other villages where he had the opportunity to impart knowledge. He sat on the board of many village councils and was the longest-serving president of the village welfare association. He considered the job of teaching very important and had a special and very noticeable passion for teaching. He was not only a great father in the community, but an amazing teacher as well. He was patient, caring, and kind. He had the ability to develop relationships with parents and students. He had knowledge of learners. He was dedicated to teaching. He was great at engaging students in learning. My luminary Papa was always prepared, known for setting clear and fair expectations, and had a positive attitude. He was very compassionate, too.

As a little girl in his class, I watched him very often feed the hungry little village kids, comfort them when they cried, and even washed those who showed up very dirty and smelly. He always had spare clothing in his school suitcase. Sometimes, I can't help but wonder if teachers like my luminary Papa inspired the African proverb "Once a teacher, always a father."

One interesting day at my village primary school was "Profession Day". It started with the Reverend Sister Mary telling us what sisterhood was all about. Next came Reverend Father Mac who told us almost the entire New Testament before concluding with what priesthood was all about. The farmer, Pa. Ndofor bored us with all we already knew about farmers. The doctor and hunter failed to show up. The day ended with my luminary Papa talking about teachers. He summarized the teaching profession into the following:

1. Teachers are people who help others, young and old, to acquire knowledge.
2. Teachers make all other professions possible.
3. Jesus Christ was the greatest teacher of all time.
4. Teaching is a gift and teachers get most of their reward from God.
5. Teachers are patient, compassionate, dedicated and honest people.
6. Teachers are great learners because you can't teach without learning.

May my luminary Papa's soul rest in peace. Amen!

What the Holy Bible says about teachers and teaching

- **James 3:1** - Not many of you should become teachers, my fellow believers, because you know that we who teach will be judged more strictly. We all stumble in many ways. Anyone who is never at fault in what they say is perfect, able to keep their whole body in check.

- **Proverbs 11:25** - A generous person will prosper; whoever refreshes others will be refreshed.

- **Proverbs 22:6** - Start children off on the way they should go, and even when they are old, they will not turn from it.

- **1 Corinthians 12:28** - And God has placed in the church first apostles, second prophets, third teachers, then miracles, then gifts of healing, of helping, of guidance, and of different kinds of tongues.

- **Titus 2:7-8** - In everything, set them an example by doing what is good. In your teaching show integrity, seriousness and soundness of speech that cannot be condemned, so that those who oppose you may be ashamed because they have nothing bad to say about us.

- **Romans 12:6-7** - We have different gifts, according to the grace given to each of us. If your gift is prophesying, then prophesy in accordance with your faith; if it is serving, then serve; if it is teaching, then teach.

CHAPTER TWENTY-NINE
SUCCESS MEANS OBEDIENCE TO GOD AND GODLY OBEDIENCE TO OTHERS

Grandma Akor was a no-nonsense granny! She was good at loving, telling funny stories, educating, and was not easily offended. To her, obedience to God and Godly obedience to others formed a solid foundation of success. One occasion by the fireside in her kitchen, one of her grandchildren, Mangwi, asked her if it was OK to go take her stepmother's food without her stepmother's knowledge or permission if the instruction was from her own mother.

Grandma gave her a suspicious look and then relaxed and said, "Mangwi, God warns us in the 8th commandment not to steal. This means you should not steal even if it means not obeying your parents or elders." She insisted that God gave Moses the ten commandments to protect us, our families as well as our communities. She then made us repeat them after her:

The Ten Commandments

1. You shall have no other gods.
2. You shall not make and worship idols
3. You shall not misuse the name of the Lord.
4. Remember the Sabbath, keep it holy.
5. Honor your father and mother.
6. You shall not murder.

7. You shall not commit adultery.
8. You shall not steal.
9. You shall not lie.
10. You shall not covet.

She cautioned that children must respect each other, show Godly obedience to parents, elders and teachers. She reminded her many grandchildren very often that:

1. An obedient child makes God happier than a hundred disobedient children.
2. Only follow your heart and mind if it is in line with God's word.
3. Always remember to obey others only if it is in conformity with the word of God, avoid blind loyalty.
4. Obedience is not always easy, but it is essential, and God blesses and rewards obedience.
5. Obedience is an act of worship.
6. Obedience demonstrates love for God and faith in Him.

What the Holy Bible says about obedience

- **Exodus 20:1-17-** And God spoke all these words: I am the Lord your God, who brought you out of Egypt, out of the land of slavery. "You shall have no other gods before me. "You shall not make for yourself an image in the form of anything in heaven above or on the earth beneath or in the waters below. You shall not bow down to them or worship them; for I, the Lord your God, am a jealous God, punishing the children for the sin of the parents to the third and fourth generation of those who hate me, but showing love to a thousand generations of those who love me and keep my commandments. "You shall not misuse the name of the Lord your God, for the Lord will not hold anyone guiltless who misuses his name. "Remember the Sabbath day by keeping it holy. Six days you shall labor and do all your work, but the seventh day is a sabbath to the Lord your God. On it you shall not do any work, neither you, nor your son or daughter, nor your male or female servant, nor your animals, nor any foreigner residing in your towns. For in six days, the Lord made the heavens and the earth, the sea, and all that is in them, but he rested on the seventh day. Therefore, the Lord blessed the Sabbath day and made it holy. "Honor your father and your mother, so that you may live long in the land the Lord your God is giving you. "You shall not murder. "You shall not commit adultery. "You shall not steal. "You shall not give false testimony against your neighbor. "You shall not covet your neighbor's house. You shall not covet your neighbor's wife, or his male or female servant, his ox or donkey, or anything that belongs to your neighbor."

▲ **Exodus 19:5** -Now if you obey me fully and keep my covenant, then out of all nations you will be my treasured possession. Although the whole earth is mine,

▲ **2 John 1:6** - And this is love: that we walk in obedience to his commands. As you have heard from the beginning, his command is that you walk in love.

▲ **Colossians 3:18–20** - "Wives, submit yourselves to your husbands, as is fitting in the LORD. Husbands love your wives and do not be harsh with them. Children, obey your parents in everything, for this pleases the LORD."

▲ **Ephesians 6:1–4** - "Children, respect and obey your parents in the Lord, for this is right."

▲ **Romans 13:1-2** - "Let everyone be subject to the governing authorities, for there is no authority except that which God has established. The authorities that exist have been established by God. Consequently, whoever rebels against the authority is rebelling against what God has instituted, and those who do so will bring judgment on themselves."

▲ **Hebrews 13:17** - Have confidence in your leaders and submit to their authority, because they keep watch over you as those who must give an account. Do this so that their work will be a joy, not a burden, for that would be of no benefit to you.

▲ **Romans12:2 - Do** not conform to the pattern of this world but be transformed by the renewing of your mind. Then you will be able to test and approve what God's will is-his good, pleasing and perfect will.

▲ **Psalm 1:1-** Blessed is the one who does not walk in step with the wicked or stand in the way that sinners take or sit in the company of mockers.

▲ **Proverbs 1:8-10 - Listen**, my son, to your father's instruction and do not forsake your mother's teaching. They are a garland to grace your head and a chain to adorn your neck. My son, if sinful men entice you, do not give in to them.

▲ **Ephesians 5:8 - For** you were once darkness, but now you are light in the Lord. Live as children of light.

CHAPTER THIRTY
IT TAKES A VILLAGE TO RAISE A CHILD

Growing up in Akum village it was not strange to be rebuked by the first elder or community member that caught you misbehaving. It was a common believe that it takes the whole village or community to raise a child because when spider webs unite, they can tie up a lion. We understood the principle of the whole village raising a child, especially since most of the elders that were quick to rebuke and punish adverse behavior from community children were also quick to feed them when they were hungry, cloth them, and provide shelter whenever necessary.

During community gatherings, the elders would most of the time greet the crowd by echoing the following, "Greetings, fellow people, when there is no enemy within us, the enemies outside cannot hurt us." And the rest of the people will answer in the dialect, "Abeli", loosely translated as "So be it". I always wondered as a little girl if this was true at all but eventually, I grew up to understand the true meaning of the power of loyalty and patriotism to one's community. The elders always talked about the importance of protecting, helping, and respecting one's community to be able to better enjoy it and leave a better legacy behind.

When one of our neighborhood kids got a scholarship to go study medicine in London, the whole community was elated. The elders all gathered in Njifor's father's compound to hand over some wisdom, to guide him through his life journey to the far away land called England. The neighborhood women cooked a variety of dishes and the men brought palm wine of different fermentation levels. The neighborhood kids were also invited to come and witness the celebration of Njifor, an upright young and valued member of the community famous for helping others, respecting others, and being a mass servant for many years.

We all gathered, and I don't know about the other kids, but I was more interested in the food than the wisdom lecture which I initially thought would be old news to me. I had parents who were experts in wisdom dissemination and imparted it very frequently and generously to us children and others who were blessed to cross paths with them.

I soon realized how wrong I was when the elders started talking. Most of what I heard from the elders that evening was new. Even all what my parents imparted for Njifor was relatively new to me. Wow! Njifor sat in the middle of her father's living room. The oldest woman in the group oiled his feet and hands with palm oil and the oldest man poured palm wine on his hands and feet. These rituals were a sign of blessing from ancestors for Njifor's well-being and prosperity. The wisdom revival highlights were as follows:

1. My son never forget where you came from. If you cut your chains, you free yourself, but if you cut your roots, you will surely and slowly die

2. Continue to be yourself, my son. Character is like pregnancy. It cannot be hidden forever.

3. Son, if you think you are too small to make a difference, you haven't spent a night with a mosquito. Go out there and make a difference!

4. Empty yourself of negative pride so you can have plenty of room for wisdom.

5. Before taking the first step, be sure you know where you are headed because if you don't know where you are going, any road will take you there.

6. Be wise always and remember, only a fool tests the depth of water with both feet.

7. Watch your tongue all the time. Only a fool says what he knows. A wise man knows what he says.

8. Be kind always for kindness is a language which the blind can see and the deaf can hear.

The evening ended with eating, drinking and dancing. Njifor returned to the village 9 years after as a medical doctor and was married to a beautiful girl from a neighboring village. He remained a role model for the neighborhood kids and shared his time and money generously.

May the soul of our community leaders rest in peace. Amen!

What the Holy Bible says about raising a child

- **Proverbs 22:6** - Train up a child in the way he should go; even when he is old, he will not depart from it.

- **Proverbs 29:15** - The rod and reproof give wisdom, but a child left to himself brings shame to his mother.

- **Proverbs 23:13-14** - Do not withhold discipline from a child; if you strike him with a rod, he will not die. If you strike him with the rod, you will save his soul from Sheol.

- **Proverbs 22:15** - Folly is bound up in the heart of a child, but the rod of discipline drives it far from him.

- **Proverbs 13:24** - Whoever spares the rod hates his son, but he who loves him is diligent to discipline.

- **Proverbs 19:18** - Discipline your son, for there is hope; do not set your heart on putting him to death.

- **Ephesians 6:1-4** - Children, obey your parents in the Lord, for this is right. "Honor your father and mother "that it may go well with you and that you may live long in the land." Fathers do not provoke your children to anger but bring them up in the discipline and instruction of the Lord.

CHAPTER THIRTY-ONE
THE POWER OF THE TONGUE

Growing up with my parents, grandma and many grand aunties and uncles was fun but, at the same time, the wisdom revival lessons were many, frequent, and overwhelming. Practically every part of the body could write a book about all that was said and being said about it. The head carried quite some notes such as "Uneasy lies the head that carried the crown", "To wear the crown, you must be able to carry one", "Just because the lizard nods its head doesn't mean it's in agreement", "The father is the head of the home", "Every head must do its own thinking", "If you fill your head with pride, you will lack space for wisdom", "Wherever the head goes, the tail follows", etc.

The eyes were a popular wisdom revival target as well. We could never get tired of hearing our parents repeat these proverbs, especially when we the children got into trouble. "What I, your grandma, can see sitting down, you cannot see standing on the tallest mountain", "It is not everything your eyes see that your mouth must be notified of", "The eye never forgets what the heart has seen", "Every closed eye is not sleeping and every open eye is not seeing". All the other body parts had their share of literature, but that will be a discussion for another day.

One body part we cannot dare ignore for later is the tongue. Oh yes, the almighty tongue! I think the tongue got us kids into more trouble than all the other body parts combined! We had some real issues with our tongues. However, when we got better with our tongues, we were punished for frowning while being rebuked or after! You don't need a tongue to frown, do you? I know perfectly well I don't need mine to frown! One of the memorable wisdom revival lectures on the power of the tongue happened one evening during our doctrine classes.

The notorious enemies Ngum and Sirche started cursing each other as soon as we got to church and found out the door was locked. Ngum, who ran to the door first, pushed Sirche who came running to open the door first. Ngum pushed her down the stairs and when she got up, she was ready to fight but was reminded we were on the church premises. They exchanged some of the worst language imaginable in the village then ("God punish you! Satan baptize you, your mother, your mother's mother! Stupid axe! Monkey head! Crocodile eyes!").

Unknown to the group of kids, the parish priest had overhead every insult and summoned the whole group into the church. He then asked Ngum whose mother was one of only two seamstresses in the whole village, "If your mother uses every bad word that comes out of your mouth to make a dress for you, how will it look?" Before Ngum even lifted her head, the notorious Sirche shouted "Leprosy!" We all laughed so hard and the whole group got into more trouble for laughing in church! We were asked to sweep and mop the whole church in one hour as punishment for cheering a fight and for laughing inside the church. After doing the punishment, the group of about 16 was then settled in the back two benches inside the church. The Doctrine Class for that evening was turned into a lecture on the power of the tongue by parish priest Father Clark:

1. You are defined by what comes out of your mouth.
2. The power of life and death lies in the tongue.
3. Be sure to taste your words before you spit them out.
4. The tongue may be soft, but it can break bones.
5. Even a fool can pass for a wise man if he knows when to shut his mouth.
6. Words are free but don't use them foolishly.

What the Holy Bible Says about the power of the tongue

- **Colossians 4:6** - Let your conversation be always full of grace, seasoned with salt, so that you may know how to answer everyone.

- **Ephesians 4:29** - Do not let any unwholesome talk come out of your mouths, but only what is helpful for building others up according to their needs, that it may benefit those who listen.

- **James 3:5** - Likewise, the tongue is a small part of the body, but it makes great boasts. Consider what a great forest is set on fire by a small spark.

- **Matthew 15:10-11** - Jesus called the crowd to him and said, "Listen and understand. What goes into someone's mouth does not defile them, but what comes out of their mouth, that is what defiles them."

- **Matthew 15:18** - But the things that come out of a person's mouth come from the heart, and these defile them.

- **Proverbs 10:19** - Sin is not ended by multiplying words, but the prudent hold their tongues.

- **Proverbs 15:4** - The soothing tongue is a tree of life, but a perverse tongue crushes the spirit.

- **Proverbs 15:28** - The heart of the righteous weighs its answers, but the mouth of the wicked gushes evil.

- **Proverbs 13:3** - Those who guard their lips preserve their lives, but those who speak rashly will come to ruin.

- **Proverbs 18:20-21** - From the fruit of their mouth a person's stomach is filled; with the harvest of their lips they are satisfied. The tongue has the power of life and death, and those who love it will eat its fruit.

- **Proverbs 21:23** - Those who guard their mouths and their tongues keep themselves from calamity.

- **Proverbs 31:26** - She speaks with wisdom, and faithful instruction is on her tongue.

- **1 Peter 3:10** - Whoever would love life and see good days must keep their tongue from evil and their lips from deceitful speech.

- **Psalm 34:13** - Keep your tongue from evil and your lips from telling lies.

CHAPTER THIRTY-TWO
A MOTHER UNDERSTANDS
WHAT A CHILD DOES NOT SAY

One of my most cherished places growing up in Akum was the village health center. Mothers will take their minor children from 0-5 years old to the clinic once a month. Going to the clinic was a big deal not only for the mothers but for the kids as well. Serious preparations were made the day before going to the clinic.

The kids had to dress in their Sunday dress and wear their clean Sunday underwear. Our mother will shower us the night before and the morning of the clinic. She will also assist us in brushing our teeth using a new chewing stick prepared the night before (usually from a guava stem) alongside some wood ash. She will then give us warm water for rinsing. The four-mile walk was usually exciting because of the anticipated goodies we would get from the clinic program.

I remember my mum carrying my baby brother on her back and holding my hand mostly through the whole journey. Once we get to the health center, the kids and the mothers had oatmeal and a glass of warm milk. After , Rev. Sister Mary Clarke who was heading the clinic program will talk about praying, hygiene, good nutrition, and the importance of sleep. She was a very beautiful woman of Irish descent and started missionary work in Africa at the age of 22. She was adored by most of us.

One of the things I loved most about Sister Mary was the fact that during one of the clinic sessions when I was just three years old, I answered most of the hygiene questions right and when she asked me what I wanted from the treasure basket, my answer was "Can I touch your hair?" She laughed and reluctantly said yes! From that day on, most of the kids that attended clinic with me were given permission to touch Sister Mary's hair when they answered a question right.

During the clinic sessions, Sister Mary and her team, mostly made up of trained young local nurses, will weigh the children, do a skin assessment, and ask the mothers questions. Children who were overweight or underweight had their mothers scheduled for an extra session. My baby brother was poster child for the clinic program and his black-and-white picture stayed on the hospital clinic wall for many, many years.

At the end of the clinic session, mothers were given a gallon of vegetable oil per family, about five pounds of brown rice per child, five pounds of powder milk per child, and about five pounds of oatmeal per child. When I turned five years old, I was given the devastating news that I had to graduate from the clinic program! OMG, I did not see that coming! I was in total shock! Sister Mary let me play with her hair one last time and gave me a big hug. I helped my sweet mother carry the goodies home and cried my eyes out throughout the four-mile walk home!

When we got home, my cute baby brother who was then about three years old tried to console me and said he could fake sick next clinic day so I could go in his spot! At least, that made me chuckle in my misery! I promised to pray hard and to fight back. I got a few friends in the neighborhood and we drafted a letter of appeal to Sister Mary. I did not let my sweet mother know about my intentions. When I went to church two days after graduation from the clinic program, I ran up to Sister Mary, greeted her, and gave her the letter of appeal!

I waited anxiously and prayed fervently for the next three weeks. When it came Friday, I kissed my cute baby brother goodbye and stayed home to clean and do laundry per my sweet mother's instructions. I did not mind at all because I knew deep in my heart that Sister Mary was going to say YES to my appeal. OMG, that was the longest wait ever! Finally, around 6 PM, I saw my cute brother running into the compound to meet me. I gave him a big hug and ran to help my sweet mother carry the goodies, which were now cut in half except the vegetable oil since my graduation from the clinic program. From the look on my sweet mother's face and the way she handed the vegetable oil to me, I immediately sensed I was in serious self-induced trouble!

I offered her a glass of gold water and was about to run out of her sight and interview my cute baby brother when she held me by the ear into the seat opposite her! I secretly wished my grandma was around to bail me out, but I was on my own! She started with "Who gave you the audacity to write a letter to Sister Mary?" Before I could even think of an answer, she continued "I got bad news for you, she said she didn't understand a thing about the letter." Whew, what a relief! Thank God! God and God alone knew what I had intended to write. For some reason, my sweet mother did not insist on knowing what I wanted to tell Sister Mary.

My apology was accepted, and I promised to never write to anyone without letting my sweet mother know. I thought that chapter was over until three weeks after, it was clinic day and my sweet mother informed me before I went to bed that Sister Mary had asked her to bring me. I was overwhelmed with gratitude. I thanked God all night and barely had any sleep. When we got to the clinic that morning, Sister Mary took me into a private room and asked what the letter was about. I explained everything to her, and she said she was going to keep me as a young mentor for the other kids and I could come every clinic day, if that's OK with my sweet mother.

My mother agreed to the terms of my new contract as a young mentor. She brought me to the clinic every first Friday of the month half-an-hour earlier than the other mothers. It was a position I enjoyed so much for two years until the clinic program ran out of funding and had to be suspended. She held my hand to the clinic and back for a while, but my heart she will continue to hold forever. My sweet mother was a true Proverbs 31 woman. She loved and feared the Lord, had virtue, strength, endurance, was charitable, provider, faithful, kind, wise, honorable, praiseworthy, and well rounded. She had the undying love of Mary, the mother of Jesus. The untiring sacrifice of Hannah, the untold influence of Jochebed, and the unfailing faith of Eunice.

May the souls of my sweet mother and Sister Mary Clarke rest in peace. Amen!

What the Holy Bible says about mothers

- **Deuteronomy 6:5-9 -** Love the LORD your God with all your heart and with all your soul and with all your strength. These commandments that I give you today are to be on your hearts. Impress them on your children. Talk about them when you sit at home and when you walk along the road, when you lie down and when you get up. Tie them as symbols on your hands and bind them on your foreheads. Write them on the doorframes of your houses and on your gates.

- **Deuteronomy 11:19 -** Teach them to your children, talking about them when you sit at home and when you walk along the road, when you lie down and when you get up. (An encouragement to obedience.)

- **Proverbs 22:6 -** Train up a child in the way he should go: and when he is old, he will not depart from it.

- **Proverbs 31:25-30 -** She is clothed with strength and dignity; she can laugh at the days to come. The speaks with wisdom, and faithful instruction is on her tongue. She watches over the affairs of her household and does not eat the bread of idleness. Her children arise and call her blessed; her husband also, and he praises her: "Many women do noble things, but you surpass them all." Charm is deceptive, and beauty is fleeting; but a woman who fears the LORD is to be praised.

- **Isaiah 66:13** - "As a mother comforts her child, so will I comfort you; and you will be comforted over Jerusalem."

- **Titus 2:3-5** - Likewise, teach the older women to be reverent in the way they live, not to be slanderers or addicted to much wine, but to teach what is good. Then they can urge the younger women to love their husbands and children, to be self-controlled and pure, to be busy at home, to be kind, and to be subject to their husbands, so that no one will malign the word of God.

CHAPTER THIRTY-THREE
SILENCE IS AN AFRICAN VALUE

I was a very talkative little girl growing up and got in a lot of trouble for either talking too much, talking at the wrong time and place, or talking at the right place and time but not saying the right things. My luminary Papa insisted that silence was a great value of self-development and spiritual growth. He reiterated often that silence was crucial when you visit a sick friend or relative and someone who has just lost a loved one. He will even advise us to take a moment of silence and think when someone annoys you. He always warned us to step aside and think before answering anyone that was in our face ready to fight. I thought it was impossible but after getting into trouble for not doing as instructed, I reluctantly obeyed the stepping aside and thinking rule and took it to a whole new level.

He also reminded me that running away from a fist fight was a mark of honor. He encouraged me to beat all my adversaries with good grades, good manners, and good hygiene. It worked, yes. I was a village kid that would not get into a fist fight but still earned bragging rights! My answer to a fist fight invitation was "See you in class during exams." He constantly encouraged me to take the time and listen and enjoy a quiet moment. He warned that if I continued talking as much as I was doing, there would be no time to think, listen, and gain wisdom. He would always give me time out to be silent and listen to myself. I thought to myself, "How funny!" If I must listen to myself, I need to be talking but my Papa insisted I had to just sit and think. Unknown to him, most of my mischievous ideas were given birth to while I was silent and thinking. Of course, a lot of good ideas also came out of my silent times.

I remember connecting more with God during those moments, too. My imagination of heaven and hell would sometimes drive me bonkers during my silent moments. I decided to focus only on good things and it really helped! After practicing silence for a while, it started giving me such a great feeling to run away from everyone and just be alone and think.

As I grew up and began to understand why my parents will occasionally set time aside to be silent, I became less suspicious of their silent moments. I finally came to the following realizations:

1. It was OK to be silent when there was nothing good to be said.
2. When people are silent, it does not mean they are angry at God, their spouse, children or friends.
3. Silence gives you the opportunity to think.
4. Silence can be a great fence around wisdom.
5. Silence screams peace.
6. He who understands your silence will understand your words even better.
7. Talk is cheap but silence can be very expensive.
8. Silence can sometimes be a good solution, but not to be used as a weapon.
9. Silence is a source of great strength.

What the Holy Bible says about the power of silence

- **Exodus 14:14 -** The LORD will fight for you; you need only to be still

- **Ecclesiastes 3:7 -** A time to tear and a time to mend, a time to be silent and a time to speak.

▲ **Romans 10:17** - Consequently, faith comes from hearing the message, and the message is heard through the word about Christ.

▲ **James 1:19** - My dear brothers and sisters, take note of this: Everyone should be quick to listen, slow to speak and slow to become angry,

▲ **Psalm 46:10** - He says, "Be still, and know that I am God; I will be exalted among the nations, I will be exalted in the earth."

▲ **Proverbs 12:23** - The prudent keep their knowledge to themselves, but a fool's heart blurts out folly.

▲ **Proverbs 17:28** - Even fools are thought wise if they keep silent, and discerning if they hold their tongues.

▲ **Lamentation 3:28** - Let him sit alone in silence, for the LORD has laid it on him.

▲ **Mark 1:12** - At once the Spirit sent him out into the wilderness,

▲ **Mark 1:35** - Very early in the morning, while it was still dark, Jesus got up, left the house and went off to a solitary place, where he prayed.

▲ **Matthew 14:13** - When Jesus heard what had happened, he withdrew by boat privately to a solitary place. Hearing of this, the crowds followed him on foot from the towns.

▲ **Job 2:13** - Then they sat on the ground with him for seven days and seven nights. No one said a word to him, because they saw how great his suffering was.

137

CHAPTER THIRTY-FOUR
NO ONE IS EXEMPTED FROM PAIN AND SUFFERING

When I was growing up, my father was usually sick, and I used to wonder why he prayed so often but wouldn't get completely healed. He went through his pain and suffering with so much integrity, grace, and courage. He was often sick but always talked about health and helping others stay healthy. One day, I gathered the audacity to ask him, "Papa, why is it that you're always sick? Why can't God heal you from your illness? And why does God allow suffering?" After a brief awkward moment of real silence, my Papa took a deep breath.

To my great relief, he answered, "My child, no one is exempted from pain and suffering. Pain and suffering are part of everyone's life: the rich, the poor, the short, the tall, those who pray, and those who do not pray." He stooped low, looked at me straight in my eyes, and added "Do you know that even doctors get sick?" He concluded by adding that long-suffering was one of the fruits of the Spirit mentioned in the Holy Bible by Paul and that even Jesus Christ who was the son of God Almighty had to suffer and die on the cross.

When I got older and understood even more, I realized all that my Papa had said about pain and suffering. I began to fully understand the benefits of pain and suffering in my own personal life. I quickly realized that suffering is a component of my authenticity as a child of God and the strongest catalyst to spiritual growth and strength. As an adult and having endured my fair share of pain and suffering, I even published a book filled with numerous accounts of pain and suffering and realized that there were amazing benefits associated with them:

1. Pain and suffering drew me closer to God and led me to repentance and salvation.
2. Pain and suffering helped me to learn important lessons in life
3. Pain and suffering eliminated the people who only tolerated me and sealed the bond with those that celebrated me
4. Pain and suffering brought creativity, resourcefulness and courage more than I could have imagined
5. Pain and suffering helped a great deal in shaping my character and humbling me
6. Pain and suffering transformed me into a champion of hope

What the Holy Bible says about pain and suffering

- **Galatians 5:22** - But the fruit of the Spirit is love, joy, peace, long-suffering, kindness, goodness, faithfulness.

- **Deuteronomy 32:10-11** - In a desert land he found him, in a barren and howling waste. He shielded him and cared for him; he guarded him as the apple of his eye, like an eagle that stirs up its nest and hovers over its young, that spreads its wings to catch them and carries them aloft.

- **Psalm 126:5-6** - Those who sow with tears will reap with songs of joy. Those who go out weeping, carrying seed to sow, will return with songs of joy, carrying sheaves with them.

- **Psalm 63:1** - You, God, are my God, earnestly I seek you I thirst for you, my whole being longs for you, in a dry and parched land where there is no water.

⋏ **2 Corinthians 1:3-5** - "Praise be to the God and Father of our LORD Jesus Christ, the Father of compassion and the God of all comfort, who comforts us in all our troubles, so that we can comfort those in any trouble with the comfort we ourselves receive from God. For just as we share abundantly in the sufferings of Christ, so also our comfort abounds through Christ."

⋏ **Isaiah 48:10** - "See, I have refined you, though not as silver; I have tested you in the furnace of affliction."

⋏ **James 1:2-4** - "Consider it pure joy, my brothers and sisters, whenever you face trials of many kinds, because you know that the testing of your faith produces perseverance. Let perseverance finish its work so that you may be mature and complete, not lacking anything."

⋏ **Job 1:13-22** - One day, when Job's sons and daughters were feasting and drinking wine at the oldest brother's house, a messenger came to Job and said, "The oxen were plowing and the donkeys were grazing nearby, and the Sabeans attacked and made off with them. They put the servants to the sword, and I am the only one who has escaped to tell you!" While he was still speaking, another messenger came and said, "The fire of God fell from the heavens and burned up the sheep and the servants, and I am the only one who has escaped to tell you!" While he was still speaking, another messenger came and said, "The Chaldeans formed three raiding parties and swept down on your camels and made off with them. They put the servants to the sword, and I am the only one who has escaped to tell you!" While he was still speaking, yet another messenger came and said, "Your sons and daughters were feasting and drinking wine at the oldest brother's house, when suddenly a mighty wind swept in from the desert and struck the four corners of the house. It collapsed on them and they are dead, and I am the only one who has escaped to tell you!" At this, Job got up and tore his robe and shaved his head. Then, he fell to the ground **in** worship and said: "Naked I came from my mother's womb, and naked I will depart. The LORD gave and the LORD has taken away; may the name of **the** LORD be praised." In all this, Job **did** not sin by charging God with wrongdoing.

⋏ **Lamentations 3:19-24 -** I remember my affliction and my wandering, the bitterness and the gall. I well remember them, and my soul is downcast within me. Yet this I call to mind and therefore I have hope: Because of the LORD's great love we are not consumed, for his compassions never fail. They are new every morning; great is your faithfulness. I say to myself, "The LORD is my portion; therefore, I will wait for him."

⋏ **2 Corinthians 12:7 -** So, to keep me from becoming conceited because of the surpassing greatness of the revelations, a thorn was given me in the flesh, a messenger of Satan to harass me, to keep me from becoming conceited.

⋏ **Philippians 1:12-14 -** Now I want you to know, brothers and sisters, that what has happened to me has served to advance the gospel. As a result, it has become clear throughout the whole palace guard and to everyone else that I am in chains for Christ. And because of my chains, most of the brothers and sisters have become confident in the LORD and dare even more to proclaim the gospel without fear.

⋏ **Hebrews 2:9-11 -** But we do see Jesus, who was made lower than the angels for a little while, now crowned with glory and honor because he suffered death, so that by the grace of God he might taste death for everyone. In bringing many sons and daughters to glory, it was fitting that God, for whom and through whom everything exists, should make the pioneer of their salvation perfect through what he suffered. Both the one who makes people holy and those who are made holy are of the same family. So, Jesus is not ashamed to call them brothers and sisters.

- **1 Peter 4:12-16 -** Dear friends, do not be surprised at the fiery ordeal that has come on you to test you, as though something strange were happening to you. But rejoice inasmuch as you participate in the sufferings of Christ, so that you may be overjoyed when his glory is revealed. If you are insulted because of the name of Christ, you are blessed, for the Spirit of glory and of God rests on you. If you suffer, it should not be as a murderer or thief or any other kind of criminal, or even as a meddler. However, if you suffer as a Christian, do not be ashamed, but praise God that you bear that name.

143

CHAPTER THIRTY-FIVE
WHEN YOU SEE SUCCESS, DON'T GET JEALOUS – GET CURIOUS

I remember one afternoon, one of the richest people in my village paid my luminary Papa a visit. They sat in our living room which we famously called "Parlor" and chatted for a long time. Papa seemed very happy and laughed very often during their visit. I always wondered why my Papa had only one wife, no car, no huge mansions but had rich friends with many wives, huge houses, and some even had more than one car. For some strange reason all these friends respected, trusted, and celebrated him. He would always remind us that we were his, pride, joy and riches! That his children were worth more than all the gold in South Africa. He cherished his children not only by his words, but by his actions as well.

Now, back to Papa and his rich friend. During the visit, he also seemed to be listening keenly. I could not wait to find out about the purpose of this rich man's visit. At least, he did not bring anything to suggest he wanted to get married to any of my older beautiful sisters, so that area was consoling. When he finally left, I was eager to ask some questions. The question-and-answer session bore the following fruits:

1. Children, hang around friends that respect themselves and respect you; friends that celebrate you, not tolerate you; friends that are honest; friends that love and fear God.
2. Dream big and believe in yourself, but plan to accumulate more memories than big dreams.

3. Never forget where you came from, always water your roots.
4. Plan on improving the lives of others.
5. Think positive, for with God, everything is possible.
6. Seize opportunities of a lifetime during the life span of those opportunities.
7. In life, some people will succeed because of their skills or talents, or failures, or death of a loved one, or education, or wisdom or a combination of any of or combination of all mentioned reasons.
8. So, whenever you meet successful people, don't get jealous because jealousy will not help you or anyone. Instead, get curious for a chance to better yourself and be of help to others.

What the Holy Bible says about successful people

- **Jeremiah 29:11**: "For I know the plans I have for you," declares the LORD, "plans to prosper you and not to harm you, plans to give you hope and a future."

CHAPTER THIRTY-SIX
SEEK CHRIST'S WISDOM, NOT KING SOLOMON'S

My luminary Papa and my sweet mother both had the wisdom of Christ. Their wisdom was both personal and professional, family-oriented wisdom and wisdom that did not compromise. Their wisdom got better with age and inspired many. The story of King Solomon and the two ladies with one baby was one of the first wisdom stories we were told as kids growing up in the village. We had a notorious song about this great story and most of us could not wait to grow up and be like King Solomon.

We were never told the whole story of the great King Solomon so one day, I gathered courage and told my father that I wanted to grow up and be a judge so I can settle disputes like King Solomon! He smiled at me and said, "My dear daughter, King Solomon was wise but not in every area of his life. Pray instead to have the wisdom of Christ that is complete and uncompromising." I really loved Jesus except I did not want to be crucified — ever! My parents showed a great deal of wisdom in what they said and did. Most of the wisdom was in our favor as their kids, but some of it was totally against what I desired.

It took me forever to understand their wisdom behind sleepovers and visiting certain family members unaccompanied. While most village kids and even our cousins could sleep over at other family members' houses, our parents prevented us from ever enjoying sleepovers, at least, that is what I thought. They would allow other children in the family to sleep over at our limited spaced house but won't allow us to sleep over at family houses some of which were as big as mansions.

We could go stay with our maternal grandmother who lived at one of our rich (but not generous) uncle's mansions. Our uncle had three wives then and many children, but our parents forbade us from sleeping over at any of the other apartments in the mansion. We were restricted to our grandmothers' section of the mansion downstairs opposite the second and third wives' kitchens.

One day out of sheer frustration, I gathered momentum and asked my Papa why we were being treated as prisoners. He giggled, pulled me closer to him, held me close to his chest, lifted my head to look into his eyes and explained, "My dearest daughter, there is so much I can do to prevent bad things happening to my family, but if I fail and something bad happens, I will not forgive myself and neither will I be able to undo the damage!" I thanked him and gathered some more momentum and took the same questions to my sweet mother and got the same answer. Not surprising to me! I think my parents were in the business of always sharing answers. We grew up well shielded from sleepovers and the good and bad that came with it. We were also shielded from meeting some family members unless we were accompanied by both of our parents or one of them. Oh yes! We were very shielded from neighbors and strangers as well.

We had one very generous uncle, husband to one of our aunties. He lived in the capital city and whenever he was in the village, his mansion was full of visitors. He entertained everyone that came into his well-fenced compound, especially family members! He was a rich and generous man and well loved by the villagers. He had a constant supply of bread, milk, rice, fried fish, drinks, canned soda (yes, canned soda for us kids!) and money.

We could never understand why our parents forbade us from ever paying him a visit even if he was in the village with our beloved aunty. Our other cousins who could visit without their parents had city candy, money, and other goodies. They will declare only some of their goodies and hide the rest, making them earn bragging rights in the neighborhood because of this. We didn't even have ownership rights over anything our uncle or aunty gave us.

As usual, it was for the entire family. It was frustrating but visiting our generous aunty and uncle behind my parent's back was not even an option worth considering. The consequences for such behavior were simply unimaginable. It was wise and better to obey, and that is just what I grudgingly did.

A year after my Papa passed away, I left high school one Sunday morning, took a cab to the village to go check on my sweet mother. I was now 18 years old and trying to deal with the passing of my Papa and being responsible and cautious. The one-hour cab ride kept me thinking just how difficult it was to go through life in the absence of my father. I prayed on the way that God will keep my sweet mother around forever, if possible!

As we approached the village junction, I noticed that my generous aunty and uncle's car was parked in their compound. Without giving it any second thought, I asked the cab driver to drop me. I paid him and rang the bell into my aunt's compound. The cook/driver opened the gate and ushered me into the living room. While in the living room, he went to notify my uncle and came out with the request that my uncle was unwell and wanted me to come see him in his bedroom. Apparently, he was in the village this time around without my lovely aunty.

I followed his driver to the bedroom, and it was my very first time going to that part of the house. I realized then that the house was much bigger than I thought. I saw my uncle in bed, not looking good at all. I gave him a hug and he held me longer than I wanted, and I couldn't wait to get out of the awkward situation. Just when I thought it couldn't get any stranger, he took my hand, kissed the back of my hand and was about to place my hand in between his thighs. I quickly pulled my hand away and ran towards the door! At the door, I stopped, came back towards the bed, looked at him in the eyes and said "I now understand why my parents protected us from you! You are a nasty old man and I will tell my mother." He replied, "Please forgive me. I don't have much time to live, protect my good name." Hearing him worry more about his good name ticked me off and I ran out of his house! It was the last time I ever saw him. He passed away two months after the incident and I laid the secret to rest, never to say anything about it to anyone.

May the souls of my luminary Papa and sweet mother rest in peace. Amen!

What the Holy Bible says about the wisdom of Solomon

Solomon was the Biblical king most famous for his wisdom. In 1 Kings, he sacrificed to God, and God later appeared to him in a dream asking what Solomon wanted from God. He wanted Wisdom. "Because you asked for wisdom, I will also give you what you did not ask for: long life, riches, and honor. You'll be greater than any other king during your lifetime." Solomon woke up and realized God had spoken to him in a dream. He became famous for his wise judgments. In one case, two women argued over a baby boy, each claiming to be the mother. Solomon ordered that the baby be cut in two and that half be given to each woman. The first woman agreed, but the real mother at once pleaded that the child be given to the other woman. Solomon now saw clearly that the compassionate woman was the mother and gave the boy to her. Soon, all Israel heard about this judicial decision, and the people recognized that the wisdom of God was within Solomon.

One of Solomon's grandest achievements was the construction of Jehovah's temple — a magnificent structure in Jerusalem that would serve as a center of worship in Israel. At the temple's inauguration, Solomon prayed: "Look! The heavens, yes, the heaven of the heavens, themselves cannot contain you; how much less, then, this house that I have built!" 1 Kings 8:27.

Solomon's reputation spread to other lands, even as far as Sheba, in Arabia. The queen of Sheba traveled to see Solomon's glory and riches and to test the depth of his wisdom. The queen was so impressed with Solomon's wisdom and the prosperity of Israel that she praised Jehovah for putting such a wise king on the throne. Indeed, with Jehovah's blessing, Solomon's rule was the most prosperous and peaceful in the history of ancient Israel. Sadly, Solomon failed to continue acting in harmony with Jehovah's wisdom. Ignoring God's command, he married hundreds of women, including many who worshipped foreign gods. Gradually his wives inclined his heart away from Jehovah to the worship of idols. Jehovah told Solomon that part of the kingdom would be ripped away from him. Only a portion would remain with his family, God said, for the sake of Solomon's father, David. Despite Solomon's defection, Jehovah remained loyal to his Kingdom covenant with David.

Issues with Solomon's wisdom

1. King Solomon had professional wisdom only.
2. King Solomon had very limited personal wisdom.
3. His wisdom was that of compromise.
4. He did not follow his own advice on women. He was recorded as having 700 wives and 300 concubines (1 Kings 11:3).

The Wisdom of Christ

Workmanship

Insights that produce results

Skill, especially technical skill

Dominion in designs that manifest God's Glory on earth

Opportunity to gain knowledge and understanding

Mastery of solutions that work

1. It is both personal and professional.
2. Unlike King Solomon, Christ's wisdom enabled him to act in harmony with Jehovah's Wisdom.
3. Unlike King Solomon, Christ's wisdom increased over time.
4. Like King Solomon, Jesus also faced temptations, but his wisdom enabled him not to fall into them.
5. The wisdom of Christ enabled him to focus on heavenly honor while Solomon, though already granted honor by God, went out seeking earthly honor through marriage to women of all tribes.

What the Holy Bible says about the wisdom of Jesus Christ

- **1 Corinthians 1:30** - But by His doing, you are in Christ Jesus, who became to us wisdom from God, and righteousness and sanctification, and redemption.

- **1 Corinthians 1:24** - But to those whom God has called, both Jews and Greeks, Christ the power of God and the wisdom of God.

- **Colossians 2:3** - In whom are hidden all the treasures of wisdom and knowledge.

- **Luke 2:40** - The Child continued to grow and become strong, increasing in wisdom; and the grace of God was upon Him.

▲ **Luke 2:52** - And Jesus kept increasing in wisdom and stature, and in favor with God and men.

▲ **Matthew 13:54** - He came to His hometown and began teaching them in their synagogue, so that they were astonished, and said, "Where did this man get this wisdom and these miraculous powers?"

▲ **Mark 6:2** - When the Sabbath came, He began to teach in the synagogue; and the many listeners were astonished, saying, "Where did this man get these things, and what is this wisdom given to Him, and such miracles as these performed by His hands?"

▲ **Revelation 5:12** - Saying with a loud voice, "Worthy is the Lamb that was slain to receive power and riches and wisdom and might and honor and glory and blessing."

CHAPTER THIRTY-SEVEN
THE RIGHTS AND RESPONSIBILITIES OF TWINS AND THEIR PARENTS

As a little girl growing up in Akum village, I prayed a lot about my future, but becoming a mother of twins was never one of my prayer intentions. However, I always secretly admired twins and the mothers of twins, especially the privileges that were associated with that. Honestly, I secretly didn't mind the responsibilities that came with the privileges of having twins in Akum village.

I never prayed nor even dreamed of becoming a mother of twins someday. But God had different plans for me and when I found out in January of 2004 that I was pregnant with twin boys, I was shocked at first. When my sweet mother reminded me of how blessed I was to be chosen amongst many women to bore a double fruit, my confusion turned into joy and gratitude!

Unlike the Chinese proverb that says, "It is not economical to go to bed early to save the candles if the result is twins," the Akum people had something different in mind. My culture, the Ngemba tribe of Akum village in the Northwest Region of Cameroon (near the West Coast of West Africa), thought twins were very economical and was almost like a case of buy-one-get-one-free. The Akum people believed twins were a special gift from God, a double blessing! The celebration of their birth in my village always involved more rituals and more varieties of food and people than 10 single births could ever pull together. Twins were the only unborn children with names already waiting for them in the Akum palace.

Once twins were born, a family member had to rush to the Akum palace to go get their names from the king. The boys will get names like Che, Fru, Nji, Forbeson, Forchi, etc. and the girls will get names like Bih, Fru, Lum, Forbeson, etc. A girl child that came after twins was Shura or Ngwe and a boy that came after twins was given the name Cho. Twin mothers had special privileges as well as responsibilities. The twins also had privileges as well as responsibilities.

1. Twins and their parents were peacemakers, problem solvers, and they acted as mediators.
2. Twins and their parents sat down before anyone else in the group took a seat.
3. Twins and their parents had the biggest piece of meat whenever there was meat sharing in the group.
4. Twins and their parents washed their hands before anyone else in the group. They also had the first and the last word in a group discussion.
5. You could not give anything to one twin without giving to the other twin and one twin could not stand when the other twin was sitting.
6. Twins were each other's keepers! When one was attacked, it meant both were fighting back.
7. Twins were the only group of people in the village that will keep their hats on when talking to the king and they will not bow down in front of the King.
8. It was common knowledge that while the king's throne was manmade, the throne of every twin was God-ordained.
9. The heads of twins were sacred! They are not to be touched or slapped or shoved. They were believed to have supernatural powers.
10. There was a traditional meal that was prepared in a special traditional pot, with special ingredients for the twins or their mothers and only eaten by the twins and their mothers.

11. There was a special grass or roots that were reserved for twins and their mothers who will wear around their heads and necks to differentiate themselves from the multitude.
12. There was a special song for honoring twins. It is sung to praise, comfort and honor them.
13. When a twin passes away, mourning would be in total silence. No gun firing.

What the Holy Bible says about twins as double blessing

- **Ecclesiastes 4:9-12** - Two are better than one because they have a good return for their labor. If they stumble, the first will lift up his friend—but woe to anyone who is alone when he falls and there is no one to help him get up. Again, if two lie close together, they will keep warm, but how can only one stay warm? If someone attacks one of them, the two of them together will resist. Furthermore, the tri-braided cord is not soon broken.

- **John 1:16** - For we have all received from his fullness one gracious gift after another.

- **Romans 9:11** - Yet, before the twins were born or had done anything good or bad in order that God's purpose in election might stand.

- **James 1:17** - All generous giving and every perfect gift is from above, coming down from the Father of lights, with whom there is no variation or the slightest hint of change.

- **Matthew 18:20** - For where two or three are assembled in my name, I am there among them.

▲ **Proverbs 27:17** - Iron sharpens iron, and one man sharpens another.

▲ **Genesis 25:22-23** - But the two children struggled with each other in her womb. So, she went to ask the LORD about it. Why is this happening to me?" she asked. And the LORD told her, "The sons in your womb will become two nations. From the very beginning, the two nations will be rivals. One nation will be stronger than the other; and your older son will serve your younger son."

CHAPTER THIRTY-EIGHT
HEAVEN HELPS THOSE WHO CAN'T HELP THEMSELVES

It was a beautiful morning the first Sunday after I received holy communion. I had gone through the tedious doctrinal classes, went to confession, and received the sacrament of holy communion. I sat with my other friends on the first pew in the church and we tried hard to behave ourselves because our parents and everybody else was watching, so we must be on our best behavior.

When we received holy communion the day before, we were each given a gift: a little notebook with interesting information. My luminary papa had set aside some money and got me my own very first Bible (the King James Version). I took my Bible and my little notebook to church that Sunday.

The church service went well as usual. The priest, who delivered the beautiful homily, concluded by saying, "Go home, children, and help yourselves, help your parents because, at the end of the day, heaven only helps those who help themselves." I went home excited and eager to read my Bible.

After going through pages and pages of the book of Matthew where the Gospel that day was based on, I was not able to find where it says, "Heaven helps those who help themselves." I decided to go to my luminary Papa for some answers. At least, he was the first person I ever knew who had a Bible. It now looked very old but still intact and well-guarded. I asked him if Matthew was the one who said that or Jesus Christ. He looked at me and after a pause, he said, "No one in the Bible said that." Before I could say anything, he added, "It is a religious doctrine discouraging laziness, but it is not a Biblical doctrine. As a matter of fact, heaven actually helps only those who can't help themselves."

What the Holy Bible says about heaven helping those who can't help themselves

- **Ephesians 2:4-5 -** But because of His great love for us, God, who is rich in mercy, made us alive with Christ even when we were dead in transgressions — it is by grace you have been saved.

- **Romans 4:4-5 -** Now to the one who works, wages are not credited as a gift but as an obligation. However, to the one who does not work but trusts God who justifies the ungodly, their faith is credited as righteousness.

- **Matthew 11:28 -** Come to me, all you who are weary and burdened, and I will give you rest.

- **Psalm 116:6 -** The LORD protects the helpless; when I was in danger, He saved me.

- **John 9:11 -** He replied, "The man they call Jesus made some mud and put it on my eyes. He told me to go to Siloam and wash. So, I went and washed, and then I could see."

- **Luke 7:11-16 -** Soon afterward, Jesus went to a town called Nain, and his disciples and a large crowd went along with him. As he approached the town gate, a dead person was being carried out — the only son of his mother, and she was a widow. And a large crowd from the town was with her. When the Lord saw her, His heart went out to her and He said, "Don't cry." Then He went up and touched the bier they were carrying him on, and the bearers stood still. He said, "Young man, I say to you, get up!" The dead man sat up and began to talk, and Jesus gave him back to his mother. They were all filled with awe and praised God. "A great prophet has appeared among us," they said. "God has come to help His people."

CHAPTER THIRTY-NINE
THE IMPORTANCE OF SEEKING WISE COUNSEL

As a little girl growing up, I always wanted to be a medical doctor. Every time a doctor came to the village for any occasion, my eyes would open wide when I heard "doctor". Whenever I was in the hospital and see a doctor, I would be so happy. Initially, I wanted to be a medical doctor and a nun. I had never seen any nun that was a medical doctor, until Reverend Sister Mary Clarke had assured me it was possible.

While in Our Lady of Lourdes all-girls secondary boarding school, I quickly realized that in order to be a medical doctor, I had to work hard on Physics, Chemistry, and Biology. I gave these three subjects my best during the first three years in secondary school. When I was moving into the fourth year, I was confident that I was going to carry on with Physics and Chemistry. There was a system in place allowing only those who scored a certain high percentage in the final Physics and Chemistry exams to carry both subjects to the next two years (Form 4 and 5). Anyone who did not make that cut was then compelled to take on Economics and Home Economics.

When I received my report card at the end of the term, I realized that I had to drop Physics and Chemistry and take on Economics and Home Economics. I was devastated! I cried my eyes out! Another dream crushed! I couldn't believe what had happened. Having this history of not fully trusting the nuns and their associates, I went to God on my knees for answers. I probably talked too much and failed to listen to God because for a long time, my questions remained unanswered. While I was waiting to hear from God, I went to my Papa for some answers. I asked him over and over why I did not make it through. His answer was simple and far from consoling, "You did not give it your utmost best."

When my father realized how disappointed I was in his answer, he went on and said to me, "My daughter, you will one day be a doctor, just not a medical doctor. The next area you are passionate about, give it your all. Go to school and keep going to school and one day, you will get a doctorate degree. You will be a Doctor of Philosophy in an area you are passionate about. With that degree and some practice and experience, you will also be able to heal people emotionally, mentally, culturally and even spiritually." My head was swelling with excitement and my heart was filling up with gratitude! He concluded by saying, "You were born with the capacity. We are grooming you with all the intent for success and all you need is God and the zeal to conquer any area you are passionate about!" Oh, my goodness, that was so consoling because I witnessed so many people come to my father for advice: doctors, priests, farmers, couples, politicians, businesspeople, students.

I thanked my Papa for his wisdom and secretly made a promise to myself to go back to school and give my best to everything I do. When I went back to school, I cooked in that cookery lab as passionately as my friends were conducting experiments in the science lab. The beauty of being in a cookery lab instead of a science lab was that while my science friends could never use me to check if their experiments were good or bad, I made good use of them tasting my cooking and helping me become a better cook. I wrote and cooked for an A grade in ordinary-level cooking. I have since excelled in my cooking, both native and western.

Today, 30 years after I had that conversation with my Papa, I come before you all with a humble spirit and a grateful heart announcing the attainment of my doctorate degree in criminal justice.

So, come to me all who labor and are heavily burdened with spiritual, leadership and criminal justice illnesses, by the grace of God Almighty, I will give ye rest - Dr. Eva

May my luminary Papa's soul continue to rest in peace. Amen!

What the Holy Bible says about seeking wise counsel

- **Proverbs 19:20 -** Listen to advice and accept discipline, and at the end, you will be counted among the wise.

- **Psalm 1:1 -** Seek not counsel from the ungodly. Seek Godly council from those season saints who you know walk with the Lord.

- **Psalm 90:12 -** So, teach us to number our days, that we may apply our hearts to wisdom.

- **Proverbs 2:11 -** Discretion will protect you, and understanding will guard you.

- **2 Timothy 3:15 -** And how from childhood you have been acquainted with the sacred writings, which are able to make you wise for salvation through faith in Christ Jesus.

- **Philippians 4:6 -** Do not be anxious about anything, but in everything by prayer and supplication with thanksgiving let your requests be made known to God.

- **Deuteronomy 6:6–7 -** And these words that I command you today shall be on your heart. You shall teach them diligently to your children and shall talk of them when you sit in your house, and when you walk by the way, and when you lie down, and when you rise.

CHAPTER FORTY
SPECIAL ACKNOWLEDGMENT

To my Amazing Goddaughter Amanda Minyui Atanga

As an 18-year-old college student, I was honored to be a godmother to one of the most beautiful babies God ever created, Amanda Atanga. She was an angel in disguise and her smile could light up a nation. Yes, a nation! The trust and humility from her parents (Uncle Livi and Aunty Feli) overwhelmed me and with a heart full of gratitude, I said yes to the offer to be a godmother without a second thought.

Later that week, I went on my knees to ask God for guidance. The answers were serious! My role in Amanda's life was going to be crucial and active. I was blessed to have a godmother who was the best any child could ask God for, so I had help already stored in my memory. However, being Amanda's godmother meant acting right all the time. What did I get myself into? The look on Amanda's cute face the day I carried her in front of all the family members and church congregation to say "Yes, I will support her parents in her walk with God" was priceless! I never ever wanted to disappoint her in any way, shape or form. I had to be a good role model for her.

Later, I moved to the USA, and kept in touch with her whenever possible. When she had to come to the USA for further studies, I was blessed to pick her up from the airport. She had matured into a beautiful, intelligent and kindhearted young lady.

And for the last ten years, we have spent quality time together and the love, trust and family bond are heavenly. She has been an amazing goddaughter and big sister to my other four kids. Being Amanda's godmother at such a young age not only prepared me for the mother I am today, but also helped in shaping my spiritual life. I will forever be indebted to Uncle Livinus and Aunty Felicia for trusting me with their precious princess and apple of God's eye, Amanda. Thank you! (Tokoh Miya.)

To my amazing goddaughter Amanda, I pray that God almighty will continue to guide, protect and provide all your needs. I appreciate your love, support, trust, and wisdom. We have laughed together, cried together, and brainstormed problems together for lasting solutions.

Adorable, amazing

Meticulous

Adventurous

Nurturing

Deserving to be loved, God-fearing

Astounding, Angel

I love and cherish you loads.

OTHER RESOURCES BY THE AUTHOR

My Letters of Gratitude to Jehovah God

Evangeline N. Asafor is originally from Cameroon near the west coast of Central Africa. As a little girl growing up, she had a dream of one day becoming an international agent of social change—a dream she thought her native country could not contain. So she migrated to the United States of America in October of 2000. One of her best days in America was the day she was sworn in as a US citizen! She made a promise to herself to be an asset to this great nation, not a liability. Evangeline has worked as a licensed practical nurse since 2004 in the areas of rehabilitation, hospice, and home health while attending school towards her greater passion of affecting social change as a criminal justice professional. One of Evangeline's worst moments in America happened when her husband was arrested for immigration irregularities, detained in Miami for eight months, and finally deported back to Cameroon. The nightmares—and God's unending presence that followed these events—prompted the writing of Letters of Gratitude. Evangeline holds a master of science degree in criminal justice and is currently pursuing a Ph.D. degree in criminal justice at Walden University.

My Sweet Mother's Doctrines of Gratitude and Her Final Rest with Jehovah God

Today it's been over three years since my sweet mother, Mama Philomena Mbuh Asafor, was called to be with Jehovah God. Though I miss her so much and will never fill the vacuum her death created in my life, her doctrines and life of godliness, gratitude, unconditional love, loyalty, struggles, integrity, resilience, and steadfastness are my vital tools for success.

Though I cannot see or touch her, I know she is near. As I listen with my heart, I am able to hear her love all around me so soft and clear. I will continue to keep my sweet mother's memories in my heart until I meet her again, nevermore to part.

It is well

God gives and God takes away. May Jehovah's name be glorified!

Gratitude as a Facilitator of Other Virtues in Jehovah God

Embrace gratitude as a worthy virtue, and the grace of Jehovah God will transform your life. Let it be your companion wherever you go, and you will reap life-sustaining benefits. Gratefulness-feeling or showing an appreciation of kindness; thankfulRecognition-acknowledgment of something's existence, validity, or legalityAppreciativeness-feeling or showing gratitude or pleasureThankfulness-expressing gratitude Indebtedness-the feeling of owing gratitude for a service or favorTeachability-able and grateful to learn God's love and insights by being taught Understanding-having insight or good judgmentDevotedness-a state of being faithfulEnthusiasm-intense and eager enjoyment, interest, or approval

REVIEWS

This book hit home with me. A true heartfelt and brave combination of struggles many of us face in all aspects of life. Evangeline has done an outstanding job of outlining her journey with this spiritual guide filled with solid principles one may use to overcome a multitude of life's challenges. Thank you for your heart felt desire to share Our Lords principles. When you start reading this book you have the urge to read non stop till the end. This book is deep. Easy read. Well written. Thank you.

— **Enaka Yembe MD.**

The author reawakens that spirit in us as she shows us how important it is to appreciate all the good and bad things that occur in our lives

— **Sheila Awahsuh**

This book is quite inspirational and exquisitely written. The spirit of gratitude is instilled in us from birth but we sometimes stray away from it due to unforeseen difficulties; however, in this book, the author reawakens that spirit in us as she shows us how important it is to appreciate all the good and bad things that occur in our lives. Great read. Embodiment of a palpable and lived relationship between father (ABBA) and daughter, Evangeline

— **Tilly. F.**

The simplicity of the dialogue between Evangeline and her Heavenly Father is inspiring. Her journey and her trust in God is palpable throughout the book. This work is not only inspiring for others going through difficult times, but a manual for any Christian along their faith journey; maintaining a close relationship with God, a complete surrender to God's will and work in your life. This book embodies and exemplifies "In all things, give God thanks" and complete trust in God. I highly recommend it! The relationship between Eva and Lord God Almighty is so beautifully displayed. What I find amazing is that she

— **Kimberly Rodriguez**

I cannot stop reading this book! It is eloquently written. The relationship between Eva and Lord God Almighty is so beautifully displayed. What I find amazing is that she shows how the same relationship is available to all through his word. The word says we will overcome by the blood of the lamb and the word of our testimony. My dear sister, YOU ARE AN OVER COMER! To God be the glory.

— **AY. D.**

A story that is beautiful, raw and heart-wrenching. Evangeline's faith touched me to the core as I read through (I highlighted phrases, sentences and at least a whole paragraph!). Her hardships are almost unreal and yet she refused to succumb to them. Somehow, she finds the will and strength to fight back and overcome. The best part is that there is a happy ending to the ordeal. Amen!! Strong and captivating read about trusting in the power of God and prayer

— **Amazon Customer**

Strong, captivating, ingenious. The writer shows resilience and walks you down a path of staying connected to God in the midst of the troubles of life. It shows us to be hopeful, trusting in the unfailing power of prayer. Excellent read!!!!!!!

— **Kindle Customer**

These letters are heartfelt , at times very sad to read but overall an amazing testimony of God's love. This is a must read for everyone who is going through a dark season in life. It is not over until its over! These testimonies have renewed and strengthened my faith in God.

Powerful letters to Jehovah God written by such a wonderful woman of God.

— **Desiree Liburdon**

Powerful letters to Jehovah God written by such a wonderful woman of God. I am so blessed to know you and call you friend. This book will truly bless your heart and serve as a daily inspiration of God's love.

I have just had occasion to peruse this artfully-presented piece ...

— **Ambe Njoh**

I have just had occasion to peruse this artfully-presented piece of literary work. It simultaneously passes for a 'how to talk to God manual' and a set of instructions on 'how to get going when the going gets tough.' The book contains many captivating and honest accounts of how its articulate and eloquent author ceded the proverbial driver's seat to the Almighty God subsequent to that fateful day when her husband was whisked away by agents of the US Immigration Service. The candor, forthrightness and reticence with which she eruditely delivers every word from the First to the seventy-forth letter is in and of itself, a feat to behold. It is a 'must-read' for anyone encountering challenges in life—and that may just as well include all breathing humans out there. Kudos, Evangeline!

— **Ambe Njoh**, University of South Florida, US

Evangeline has done a great job in a simple but well-written epistle of her ...

— **Princess Trillon**

This book was very refreshing to read. It brought faith and prayer alive as I read every page. You could feel every pain, join in on every prayer and join in the hope that resided in the mind of its writer. Evangeline has done a great job in a simple but well-written epistle of her struggles many of which mothers, couples, parents, immigrants, and Christians can relate to. You have done your maker and your family proud.

This book is great! It shows the power of thanksgiving

— **Olivia**

This book is great! It shows the power of thanksgiving. It portrays thanksgiving as a tool for spiritual growth, an instrument of praise, an approach to putting challenges in perspective, an inspiration for strength through Faith, and a weapon against evil. I would recommend this book because it connects the reader into a personal relationship with God as a heavenly Father.

Brings personal relationship with God to limelight

— **FELIX OMORODION**

Personal life story totally linked to her very strong Faith in God. These are series of personal communications with God almighty something everyone should learn from her perusal experiences with Jehovah.

I highly recommend reading the book but also learn from the amazing power of God.

— **His Royal highness Felix Omorodion.**

Oh, the wrench of a mother's heart at the ...Oh, the wrench of a mother's heart at the thought of tomorrow's uncertainty! What an inspirational book for all God's creations. Every page jolted my heart. I'm inspired and know to keep walking in faith. The fight is never over until God says so. Amen! This book is very powerful and a great read. It shows the power of God in ...

— **Amanda**

This book is very powerful and a great read. It shows the power of God in our lives, and confirms that indeed, God will never take you where He will not guide you! Kudos and Godspeed!

A truly inspiring tale of woman that has sacrificed everything ...

— **Tommy Saltoon**

A truly inspiring tale of woman that has sacrificed everything for her family. Motivational, awe-inspiring , a must-read !!!

An inspiring and touching memoir..... ...

— **Francis Ntumngia**

An inspiring and touching memoir....... the life and struggles of a wife and mother.......and the power of faith and trust in God.

— **Josie Mama**

Very inspiring. I love the communication with God through letters. Great writing sr Evans... I am really proud of you.

— **Anje Makia**

What a unique way of writing a book! Worth reading more than once! God will tell me who you really are as I continue to search the source of your wisdom. Ride on and pull us along. You have given me all assurance that everything comes at the appointed time. I am glad you speak a language that I understand so well. Go and do His work daughter of the Almighty.-

— **Mummy Flo**

I'll discover this special book about a special person particularly close to my heart with great pleasure.

— **PA'A ASAFOR.**

Hi, Evan!

You turned your mother's advices into a deeply moving memoir! Wahoo!! Congratulations!!!

— **James Conable**

I will do! I finished the book and it was lovely! I know even more that your mother was one special Godly lady!

— **Janis Small**

I read your Letters of Thanksgiving book. Wow. Heart rending yet inspiring. I'm in awe of you, you super woman you! Thanks for sharing your story with the world. Keep shinning, keep soaring! Lots of love...xxx

— **Carine Teche**

Dearest Sis Eva. Thank you for sharing your life with us today. You are mighty in the Spirit. You touched many lives and gave many hope today. The Lord has preserved you well through the storms of life. Continue to dwell in the secret place of the most high. Blessings.

— **Elder Marcel**

Hi Dr. Evangeline, thanks for sharing. I read the 2 books on my way to Nigeria and both of them are WHEW! I greatly enjoyed the lessons on gratitude from Mama a lot. May God continue to strengthen your hand to bless your world. Kindly forward the link to the site where the books were publish.

— **Dr. Kunle**

Sweetheart I started reading your book today, it's so inspirational that I see it done thru the weekend. Thanks for sharing such insights of your life. Papa God thank you for making Evans for me.

— **Cathy Ngassa**

Greetings my dear Sis, I pray you got home to FL safely. What a joy to have met you and be furnished with your powerful testimony. I am reading the 11th Letter and being enriched, challenged and blessed with its simplicity. In fact, a child talking to her Father. Profound! Who can beat that? To be frank, I am learning how to have a heart of gratitude as I read. Rather than "it's a right" kind of gratitude with Our Father. Sis thank you for sharing your story with the world. May He continue to inspire you with deeper and transforming revelations. Amen

— **Sis Monique Ndikum**

Started reading your book it brought back so many memories. You touch my heart! Thank you for letting us be part of yesterday...

— **Pastor Dale**

Thank you. And may everything be right back to you may your day and your week be blessed. Love you. Enjoying your book. Wow what faith you have.

— **Esther**

Your faith, hope and love for your family and for God is profound. You have been tried with the fuller's instruments and shines better than gold. The Lord bless you more and more in His comforts and lead you deeper into his knowledge, influence, grace and fulfilment of eternal joy in His Provisions to save many as the light of this world

— **Albert Uduma**

Just finished reading your book. Woah! your God is special Girl you had resilience. It was as if hell Was breaking loose on you but you didn't give up. If I hear Akum them call ya name again, you go hear say I don fight for Minnesota. Your story was inspiring and empowering. Woah! Ashia mami, you did it.

Hi Evangeline, I read your book in one sitting and I want to tell you that it shoke me to the core. You showed a totally different perspective on life. I don't thank Jesus enough for my blessings. I should begin the day with a gratitude to Him, always. Thank you for showing me this positive way to live. I am very grateful to you.

— **Maria k.**

IEM PRESS

To order additional copies of this book
or to check out our other quality custom-published books,
call 317-975-0806
or visit www.iempublishing.com

"Inspiring, equipping, and motivating — one author at a time."

www.ingramcontent.com/pod-product-compliance
Lightning Source LLC
Chambersburg PA
CBHW071203160426
43196CB00011B/2176